Business Ethics:
A Jewish Perspective

Moses L. Pava

Associate Professor of Accounting and
Alvin Einbender Chair in Business Ethics
Sy Syms School of Business
Yeshiva University

KTAV PUBLISHING HOUSE, INC.
YESHIVA UNIVERSITY PRESS

Library of Congress Cataloging-in-Publication Data

Pava, Moses L.
    Business ethics : a Jewish perspective / Moses L. Pava.
        p.   cm. — (The Library of Jewish law and ethics : v. 21)
    Includes bibliographical references and index.
    ISBN 0-88125-582-3
    1. Economics—Religious aspects—Judaism. 2. Business ethics. 3. Ethics, Jewish.
I. Title. II. Series.
    BM509.E27P38   1997
    296.3'644—dc21   97-2737
                                                                                CIP

Manufactured in the United States of America

To my parents,
my first and best teachers

Contents

Acknowledgments

The assumption of this book is that traditional Jewish thought not only provides inspirational guidance in our personal lives, but may also inform our understanding of appropriate business behavior. Many of us spend more than forty hours a week in a business environment. Is the sole objective really the maximization of profits, as economists would have us believe? The integration of Jewish ethical teachings with the best of secular business texts offers an opportunity to enhance the meaningfulness of our working lives. It is hoped that this book will find a wide audience among business men and women, students, and academics. To this end, the book is jargon-free.

The book was inspired by my many students at the Sy Syms School of Business, Yeshiva University. The agenda was set by their intelligent questions and comments. In my numerous formal and informal conversations with them, my students have demonstrated curiosity, intellectual rigor, and a deep faith in Judaism. They continually demand an answer to the question of how best to integrate the worldviews of religion and business. They realize that we are beyond the point where we can ignore such questions. This book is my attempt at a coherent and thoughtful response. It is not meant to be the last word on the subject, but rather the continuation of an ongoing discussion.

I am grateful to Dean Harold Nierenberg for providing an environment conducive to seeing this project through to its conclusion. In addition, I thank the President of Yeshiva University, Dr. Norman Lamm, the Vice President of Academic Affairs, Dr. William Schwartz, and the Assistant Vice President, Jeffrey Gurock, for their continued support and helpful encouragement.

Numerous colleagues have provided useful feedback in one form or another. Aaron Levine, both through his numerous writings and hours of conversation with him, has provided a model of integrity and intellectual precision in the area of Jewish business ethics. I have also benefited much from extended discussions with Benzion Barlev, Moshe Bernstein, Phil Miller, Kalman Newman, Patrick Primeaux, Mickey Rosen, and J. J. Schachter. Clarence Walton, often acknowledged as the father of business ethics, continues to serve as a mentor and guide. His timely responses and deep wisdom have had an enormous impact on my thinking. His actions, always characterized as *lifnim mishurat hadin* ("beyond the letter of the law"), provide practical models to emulate. In addition, I wish to thank all of the publishers who granted me permission to quote from their books.

As always, I thank my wife, Vivian Newman, for her love, companionship, and intuitive grasp of the issues discussed in this book. Although she may not agree with every statement, she has participated fully in their formulation. She is my strongest and best critic.

Finally, this book is dedicated to my father and mother, Samuel and Beverly Pava. In their personal, family, and communal lives, they constantly prove the beauty and practicality of Jewish ethics. Their unmatched faith and untiring efforts as Jewish lay leaders in Springfield, Massachusetts, and Kodimoh Synagogue reveal the best of our Jewish heritage. Their relationship to one another, to their family, to the Jewish community, and to the community at large is infused by an incredible devotion and love. It is this love which is the heart and soul of Jewish ethics, business or otherwise.

Moses L. Pava
Jerusalem, Israel

Foreword

The growing literature on business ethics often leaves the business practitioner who aspires to ethical standards frustrated and unhappy. Much of what he/she reads appears irrelevant or at best remote to him, even if it is, in its own way, intellectually interesting. Yet he craves ethical guidance, some way to give moral credibility to his life and his preoccupations and "connect" his mundane life with his spiritual aspirations.

The situation calls to mind the Biblical Jacob who dreamt of a ladder extending from heaven to earth, with angels ascending and descending on it. Had the ladder been merely from one point to another in heaven, the angels would have been going only in one direction—up—or there would have been no need for them at all. But the ladder was firmly planted on earth, even while its top reached heaven. That is why the angels went both up and down.

All this is but a metaphor for the truism that any real, livable, meaningful ethic must be the result of the conjunction of the ideal and the real, the heavenly and the earthly, the theoretical and the practical. The only way to attain the transcendent Jewish ideal of *kedushah*, saintliness, is by connecting both heaven and earth, by recognizing that one's conduct rises above the mundane and the profane only when the angels can go down as well as up, when they bring our ideals into the mainstream of our daily pursuits and then, tested by "reality," elevate them to *kedushah*.

Professor Pava, whose family I have known for three genera-tions long before he joined the faculty of Sy Syms School of Business/Yeshiva University, here presents us with an exciting and eminently readable work ("jargon-free," as he calls it) in which exalted ideas are challenged by facts on the ground, and the quotidian affairs that so absorb us are elevated by a religiously inspired and formulated legal-ethical awareness. In both content and style, he explains the relevance and applicability of Judaism's halakhic prescriptions and its moral vision as they relate to the realities of the business person's practical life. Our author's work is but the latest example of the philosophy of *Torah Umadda*, the synergy of traditional Jewish learning and worldly wisdom, that is the guiding spirit of Yeshiva University.

It is a pleasure to include this important volume as the latest in the Yeshiva University/KTAV Library of Jewish Law and Ethics—another rung in our literary Jacob's ladder.

Norman Lamm

1

Introduction: An Integrative Framework

Business managers, board members, employees, shareholders, consumers, government regulators, and social critics are increasingly aware of the importance of and need for a well-developed business ethics. Even a casual reading of our daily newspapers and weekly news magazines suggests that failures in business ethics are rampant. Consider for a moment just one example. A recent *Business Week* cover story (Oct. 23, 1995) focused on some questionable business decisions at Bausch & Lomb. The author of the article, Mark Maremont, reported the following items related to the company:

1. In the late 1980s and early 1990s, Hong Kong was the star of Bausch & Lomb's international division, often racking up annual growth of 25 percent as it rocketed to about $100 million in revenues by 1993. Trouble was, in recent years, some of the reported sales were fake (p. 47).

2. Nowhere did the situation get more out of hand than in the U.S. contact-lens division. Lacking a disposable lens to counter Johnson & Johnson, the unit tried a shortcut. Starting in 1989, it took the same lenses sold since the 1970s and repackaged them as the frequent-replacement Sequence 2 and Medalist brands. But

while a pair of the older Optima lenses went for about $70, the new brands went for as low as $7.50 (p. 51).

3. By accepting cash payments and third-party checks, a Miami warehouse may have indirectly helped launder drug money until mid-1990. Senior Bausch & Lomb managers tolerated the lucrative trade, say former executives (p. 47).

The *Business Week* article suggests that these and other ethical lapses, far from representing isolated incidents (as chief executive officer Daniel E. Gill would have us believe), were pervasive at Bausch & Lomb. The questionable behavior, which included extremely dubious accounting practices, an attempt to fool consumers to get them to pay exorbitant prices for the company's products, and little concern for the welfare of the local communities in which the company engaged in commerce, was the result of an organizational philosophy which emphasized short-run financial goals to the exclusion of other corporate responsibilities. According to former executives at the company, the corporate culture was driven almost exclusively by the numbers. The most important goal was "double-digit annual growth" (p. 48).

One solution to the problems discussed above is increased government regulation. The argument seems to be that the best way to reduce the problems associated with business is to reduce the ability of men and women to do business. Removing choices from business decision makers and transferring it to government regulators and bureaucrats will leave business managers less opportunity to manipulate markets and engage in questionable activities. Certainly, there is a place for government regulations, but big-government solutions seem less appealing in an era marked by intense suspicion of political leaders. Critics of big government point out the often dramatic inefficiencies in many government programs. A program as well intended as minimum wage legislation ends up hurting those it is specifically designed to help. The minimum wage is indeed raised, but at the cost of increased unemployment among the economically weakest members of society. Critics also frequently point out that as the size of government increases relative to the business sector, the opportunity for the agents of government to engage in questionable behavior is enlarged. Many view our current predicament as a no-win situation. Cynicism toward business and governmental leaders is a common symptom of our age. Is there an alternative to cynicism?

Surely, most of us recognize, if only intuitively, that our own economic and material well-being, and that of our children and grandchildren, is dependent on the spiritual values, norms, and principles which define us. Significantly, Adam Smith, the author of *The Wealth of Nations* and the father of modern economics, explicitly recognized this in his less famous, but no less important book, *The Theory of Moral Sentiments*. Smith pointed out that "Men could safely be trusted to pursue their own self-interest without undue harm to the community not only because of the restrictions imposed by the law, but also because they were subject to built-in restraint derived from morals, religious custom, and education" (as quoted by Hirsch 1976, p. 137). Smith's insight is important, even if it has usually been difficult to appreciate its true significance. Historically, it has been easier to understand that technological breakthroughs leading to new products and new technologies ultimately increase our material satisfaction. Only more recently has the link between "ethical breakthroughs" and economic output been fully appreciated. To Adam Smith, writing in the eighteenth century, it probably did appear that moral and religious restraints were "built-in." On the verge of the twenty-first century, we will be forgiven if we question this assumption. We are well beyond the point where we can assume an automatic acceptance of a universally known ethical code. As business organizations grow beyond our wildest imaginings, it becomes ever more urgent to understand explicitly the role of business in society, to articulate carefully the social responsibilities of business organizations, and to painstakingly identify the moral demands of the individual.

The purpose of this book is to explore and interpret Jewish religious writings in light of contemporary business ideology and practice. The book investigates both traditional teachings and modern Jewish voices. A conscious attempt is made to integrate the best of the ever growing academic business literature with authoritative Jewish sources.

The approach adopted here suggests that it is not enough to offer pietistic and moralistic warnings. A self-righteous catalogue of additional and ever more restrictive prohibitions cannot but grow dusty sitting on a bookshelf. Business men and women are often highly intelligent and among the most creative individuals around. They are committed to producing high-quality, socially useful products at low costs. Business men and women enjoy a well-deserved sense of accomplishment by providing others with creative employment opportunities. Entrepreneurs create work communities that often endure for decades, or even longer. Michael Novak (1982, p. 17) reminds us of the central role that business has played in vastly improving our lives.

> The invention of the market economy in Great Britain and the United States more profoundly revolutionized the world between 1800 and the present than any other single force. After five millennia of blundering, human beings finally figured out how wealth may be produced in a sustained, systematic way. In Great Britain, real wages doubled between 1800 and 1850, and doubled again between 1850 and 1900. Since the population of Great Britain quadrupled in size, this represented a 1600 percent increase within one century. The gains in liberty of personal choice—in a more varied diet, new beverages, new skills, new vocations—increased accordingly.

Writing about business ethics must begin with at least one eye focused on "how wealth may be produced." If business men and women are left out of the business ethics "debate," the substance and quality of the discussion will suffer. It is well to keep in mind Andrew Stark's often-quoted criticism of academic business ethics. Writing in the prestigious *Harvard Business Review*, Stark (1993, p. 38) noted,

Far too many business ethicists have occupied a rarified moral high ground, removed from the real concerns and real-world problems of the vast majority of managers. They have been too preoccupied with absolutist notions of what it means for managers to be ethical, with overly general criticisms of capitalism as an economic system, with dense and abstract theorizing, and with prescriptions that apply only remotely to managerial practice.

While Stark's critique was mainly targeted at purely secular approaches to business ethics, it often applies equally well to religiously grounded business ethics. An approach divorced from the realities and material needs of a modern, pluralistic society is of no help to anyone.

The tension created by the integrative approach adopted in this book cannot be denied. It is the hope and faith of the author that such tension is ultimately rewarded with creative and innovative solutions to seemingly intractable problems. Norman Lamm (1990, p. 236), the president of Yeshiva University, and the most eloquent and articulate spokesman for the integrative approach (which he labels *Torah U'Madda*), has described its possible benefits in the form of an adaptation of the concept of complementarity in modern physics:

Complementarity offers rousing support to the comprehensiveness of the whole approach. Torah, faith, religious learning on one side, and Madda, science, worldly knowledge on the other, together offer us a more overarching and truer vision than either set alone. Each set gives one view of the Creator as well as His creation, and the other a different perspective that may not at all agree with the first. Yet, "they are given from one Shepherd," as Ecclesiastes (12:11) taught. Each alone is true, but only partially true; *both together present the possibility of a larger truth, more in keeping with the nature of the Subject of our concern* [emphasis added].

Following Lamm, this book will have been successful if it can demonstrate that Jewish sources provide significant insights to help us understand and better formulate a realistic approach to business.

The core problem of business ethics is how best to accommodate the often-conflicting need for individual freedom with the constant demand for responsibility. Business men and women require the freedom to experiment. Incentives must be in place to ensure investments in research and development. Business men and women need to be able to raise and lower prices. Businesses must be able to hire and fire employees. They need to protect proprietary information. Yet, at the same time, Jewish ethics uncompromisingly insists that men and women are "created in the image of God" and are commanded to emulate His ways.

Each chapter of this book explores some aspect of the conflict between the authentic need for freedom and the deeply felt requirements of responsibility. In each chapter, tentative solutions are offered. It should be emphasized that the thoughts expressed here are not meant to be final or definitive. Rather, the modest hope is that this book can provoke further discussion and search within the integrative framework.

Specifically, the book is divided into three parts. Part I asks and attempts to answer the question of why we often fail at business ethics. The thesis offered in chapter 2 is that decision makers fail to consider the logic of decision making. Most business curriculums teach students to view decisions almost exclusively as opportunities to maximize self-interest. In many cases this strategy is well warranted. But like any ideology, when taken to an extreme, the ideology of rational decision making can lead to perverse and undesirable results. Important business decisions can also be "framed" as religious and ethical decisions. Decision making provides opportunities to explore issues of identity and to seek personal and communal meaning.

In Part II, given the desire to move beyond the view of human behavior as being motivated by pure self-interest, the book carefully examines the foundations of a Jewish business ethics. Chapter 3 introduces and discusses three goals of a Jewish business ethics. The emphasis here is on introducing some of the important biblical, talmudic, and post-talmudic texts that deal with business ethics. As the discussion will show, Judaism's traditional texts deal with an amazing variety of issues emphasizing responsibilities in the business context. These texts are both legalistic and aspirational. An important theme of the chapter is that an authentic Jewish business ethics must grow out of an understanding of the needs of modern, complex economies but need not accept the status quo as binding. Jewish business ethics texts provide rules of behavior, but more importantly, they reveal a vision encouraging us to incorporate the highest human and spiritual ideals into the ordinary world of business. The chapter is inspired, in large measure, by Rabbi Joseph B. Soloveitchik's path-breaking essay, *The Lonely Man of Faith* (1965), in which he emphasized the Bible's two distinct descriptions of man's creation.

Chapter 4 continues and extends the discussion through an analysis of the substance of Jewish business ethics. The chapter asks, What sense is there in speaking about a business ethics particular to Judaism? Just as a Jewish algebra or a Jewish physics is a contradiction in terms, so too, perhaps, is the notion of a peculiarly Jewish business ethics. This proposition is vigorously denied. It will be argued that Jewish business ethics, in terms of substance, differs from secular approaches in three very specific ways. Jewish ethics (1) recognizes God as the ultimate source of value, (2) acknowledges the centrality of the community, and (3) holds out the promise that men and women (living in community) can transform themselves. In contrast, secular approaches need make no assumptions about the existence or nonexistence of God, generally (although certainly not always) start with the idea of the isolated individual as fundamental, and make no a priori claims about the unique potential of man and the community for transformation.

Finally, in chapter 5, the discussion turns from issues of substance to issues of methodology. If we claim to be studying Jewish business ethics, what is it that we are doing? How do we proceed? In answering these questions an important characteristic of religious ethics, and more particularly Jewish ethics, emerges. The uniqueness of a Jewish business ethics hinges as much on the method of inquiry as on the substance of the inquiry. The chapter draws heavily from both traditional Jewish sources and the work of Michael Walzer. The chapter suggests that the method of interpretation offers the best hope for solutions to contemporary business problems and is consistent with the way most of us actually "do" business ethics. It is too late in the game for new discoveries, and attempts at ethical invention are illusions. Those who walk the path of interpretation believe that even before they begin the search, they already live in a moral world. The very process of searching for moral principles makes sense only if one assumes at the outset a preexisting morality. Interpreting human institutions or literary and religious texts requires looking backwards and seeing where we have been and why we have been there. It is only in looking backwards and answering these question that one can rationally proceed to ask, "Where should we be going?" The chapter concludes by noting that the path of interpretation is consistent with, and promotes the substance of, Jewish ethics, as discussed in chapter 4. Method and substance complement one another.

Part III focuses on some of the more practical aspects of a Jewish business ethics. It applies the theoretical discussion of Part II to various issues of concern to business practitioners. The focus of chapter 6 is the controversial issue of corporate social responsibility. At least two major perspectives on social responsibility can be isolated. The classical view, most closely identified with Milton Friedman, suggests that social responsibility is incompatible with a free enterprise economy. By contrast, advocates of increased social responsibility point out the desirability of voluntary (and at times costly) corporate activities that promote society's well-being. The purpose of chapter 6 is to briefly describe both the classical and the pro–social responsibility perspectives. We suggest that while important differences in assumptions characterize the two distinct views, there is enough overlap and agreement to move the debate beyond the current stalemate. Specifically, we argue that the concept of *lifnim mishurat hadin,* an innovative and ancient Jewish legal doctrine which is usually translated as "beyond the letter of the law," might serve as a model for modern legal and social thought.

Chapter 7 highlights issues related to "inside information." Specifically, the purpose of the chapter is to examine and understand two important events in the life of the biblical figure of Joseph in light of recent economic theory. By focusing on the economic concept of inside information and other economic insights, a new, albeit experimental view of the Joseph narrative emerges. The inclusion of this material demonstrates the need for a religious ethics to move beyond purely legalistic approaches. Religious narrative can be an important source from which business men and women draw both inspiration and intellectual models.

Finally, chapter 8 concludes with the suggestion that Jewish business ethics should be treated as a practical rather than a theoretical enterprise. The initial question for Jewish business ethics is not a hypothetical one about how business would be conducted in an ideal halakhic world, but rather how Jewish teachings can inform the business ethics debate, given the realities of the modern situation. If this approach is correct, the study of Jewish business ethics becomes not only an academic exercise but, ideally, a source of useful models for business men and women to emulate.

The argument in chapter 8 proposes that we need to confront the issue of pluralism head-on. Given the reality that neither the state nor the corporation is a Torah institution, what role is there for religious values to play? The traditional answer has been that religious teachings can guide the individual business man or woman, but have virtually no role to play at the level of the organization or state (at least given current political and social conditions). This final chapter suggests that another, very different answer is possible. Religious sources, and in particular Jewish sources, can teach us much about how business enterprises should be organized. The realities of pluralism do not necessarily entail the rejection of traditional teachings. Quite the contrary, a return to and an appropriate interpretation of our ethical inheritance are necessary first steps to the continued development of a flourishing pluralistic society.

What the Bausch & Lomb case cited earlier suggests, above all, is that business executives need a more precise and expansive language with which to conduct business. An all-encompassing focus on financial outcomes to the exclusion of other corporate actions is insufficient. Business executives need to incorporate ethical language. Jewish texts provide an untapped source of wisdom, integrity, and practical idealism.

PART I

Background

And he took the book of the covenant, and read in the ears of the people: and they said, "All that the Eternal has spoken, we will do, and we will listen (*na'aseh v'nishma*)."   (Exodus 24:7)

When the Israelites gave precedence to "we will do" over "we will hearken," a heavenly voice went forth and exclaimed to them, "Who revealed to My children this secret which is employed by the ministering angels?"   (Shabbat 88a)

There was a certain Sadducee who ... exclaimed, "Ye rash people who gave precedence to your mouth over your ears: ye still persist in rashness. First ye should have listened, if within your powers, accept, if not, ye should have not accepted." Said Raba to him, "We who walked in integrity, of us it is written, `The integrity of the upright shall guide them ...'"   (Shabbat 88a)

2

Why We Fail at Business Ethics and How We Might Succeed

In 1982, Bowen McCoy, an investment banker with Morgan Stanley, enjoyed a rare opportunity. He was the first participant in the bank's new six-month sabbatical program. He spent the first half of the sabbatical in Nepal, "walking 600 miles through 200 villages in the Himalayas and climbing some 120,000 vertical feet" (McCoy 1983, p. 191). His only Western companion was an anthropologist friend named Stephen.

The high point of the expedition occurred halfway through the Himalayan part of the trip. McCoy and his companions faced an 18,000-foot pass over a crest that they would have to climb to reach Muklinath, an ancient holy place for pilgrims. On an earlier expedition McCoy had experienced severe altitude sickness at only 16,500 feet. He was naturally both apprehensive and excited about the prospect of traversing the pass. By his own account, McCoy considered the climb "a once in a lifetime trip." On the day before McCoy and Stephen were to attempt the climb, at about 14,500 feet, they were joined by a group of four climbers from New Zealand. In addition, Japanese and Swiss groups were not far below.

Finally, the day of the ascent arrived. At about 15,500 feet, Stephen and some of the porters accompanying them began to show signs of altitude sickness. The Sherpa guide became ever more anxious about the group's ability to get across the pass. It was at this point that the hikers suddenly faced an excruciatingly difficult ethical dilemma. In retrospect, McCoy described the situation as follows:

> Just after daybreak, while we rested at 15,500 feet, one of the New Zealanders, who had gone ahead, came staggering down toward us with a body slung across his shoulders. He dumped the almost naked, barefoot body of an Indian holy man—a sadhu—at my feet. He had found the pilgrim lying on the ice, shivering, and suffering from hypothermia. I cradled the sadhu's head and laid him out on the rocks. The New Zealander was angry. He wanted to get across the pass before the bright sun melted the snow. He said, "Look, I've done what I can. You have porters and Sherpa guides. You care for him. We're going on!" He turned and went back up the mountain to join his friends. (p. 193)

After taking the sadhu's pulse and determining that he was still alive, McCoy, concerned about his own ability to function at this altitude, immediately proceeded toward the summit without Stephen. Again, his own words are worth quoting: "Without a great deal of thought, I told Stephen and Pasang [the Sherpa guide] that I was concerned about withstanding the heights to come and wanted to get over the pass. I took off after several of our porters who had gone ahead" (p. 193). After McCoy abruptly left, Stephen tried to persuade Pasang to order some of the porters to carry the sadhu to a lower altitude, but Pasang resisted the idea, arguing that the porters would need all of their remaining strength to get over the pass themselves. Stephen also tried to persuade the Japanese party to let him borrow their horse to transport the sadhu to a lower altitude, but the members of this party also refused. Stephen, in deep despair, finally left the sadhu lying on the ground listlessly throwing rocks at the Japanese group's dog. To this day, neither Stephen nor McCoy knows if the Indian holy man is alive or dead.

McCoy's "parable" embodies many characteristics of the classic business ethics dilemma. For this reason the case is worth studying extensively. As typically happens in business, problems, ethical or otherwise, arrive unexpectedly and require an immediate response. It is almost impossible to predict the arrival of a true ethical dilemma, and pushing off a decision is often impossible. Like the sadhu, ethical problems are "dumped" at our feet and require immediate attention.

Further, ethical problems in business often arise because of a lack of clarity as to precisely who within a group is responsible for a particular situation. The *Exxon Valdez* disaster, for example, highlights a number of interesting questions about responsibility for corporate actions. Can managers and shareholders at Exxon simply argue that Captain Joseph Hazelwood, who was legally drunk when he was tested more than ten hours afterwards, was solely responsible for the wreck? To what extent is the third mate Gregory Cousins, the individual who actually steered the vessel onto the submerged rocks, culpable? Does the Coast Guard, which failed to detect the wandering ship, bear any responsibility? Corporate actions involve the cooperative efforts of numerous individuals. Because of this it is often extremely difficult to assign ethical responsibility while a dilemma is being faced, or even in retrospect. In the case of the sadhu, McCoy suggests that no one individual working alone could have saved him. An adequate solution required a group effort.

Third, as in business, McCoy and his fellow hikers were involved in pursuing a superordinate goal. The very purpose of their mission was universally perceived to be reaching the summit. In the business context, the superordinate goal is thought to be profit maximization. Ethical actions and solutions often require the group to postpone or lower previously sought goals, even where substantial investments of time and money in pursuit of the goal have been incurred.

Finally, business dilemmas are ambiguous. Not only do they arrive unexpectedly, but when they do arrive, they bear no labels. As McCoy himself correctly notes, "Real moral dilemmas are ambiguous, and many of us hike right through them, unaware that they exist" (p. 196).

McCoy and his fellow hikers, high on adrenaline and expectation, unexpectedly and inadvertently stumbled into an ethical dilemma. To be sure, at the time, the hikers failed to recognize it as such. Their inability to adequately meet the needs of the helpless Indian holy man parallel many of today's modern business failures. The purpose of this chapter is to examine the causes for these breakdowns. Why do we fail at business ethics? A plausible answer to this question might help us to avoid future ethical traps.

A Problem of Framing

The thesis of this chapter is that many business ethics failures are caused by an inability to define the decision context appropriately. Decision makers fail to consider the logic of decision making. Most business curriculums teach students to view decisions almost exclusively as opportunities to maximize self-interest. In many cases this strategy is well warranted. But like any ideology, when taken to an extreme, the ideology of rational decision making can lead to perverse and undesirable results.

Important business decisions can also be framed as religious and ethical decisions. Decision making provides opportunities to explore issues of identity and to seek personal and communal meaning. Although attempts have been made to show how religious and ethical decisions are consistent with a pure logic of consequence, ultimately the unique characteristics of these kinds of decisions do not easily fit into the dominant business ideology. Business decisions will finally be improved by understanding and examining the ambiguities associated with corporate decision making and searching for better ways to resolve them. Ethical dilemmas are never well defined and rarely well understood. Treating ethical dilemmas as "ordinary" decisions is often tantamount to ignoring them, and ignoring them inexorably leads to business ethics failures.

The Uses and Limits of the Rational Model

The rational model of decision making is an extremely important tool for business managers. The thesis discussed here in no way calls for the jettisoning of the rational model. Rather, it is necessary to view the rational model in its proper context as one tool of decision making among others.

James March, in *A Primer on Decision Making,* has provided a comprehensive description of the rational model. In March's view, standard theories of choice always assume that decision processes are both *consequential* and *preference-based.* Decisions about taking actions are dependent on the anticipated consequences of the actions. Decision processes are preference-based in the sense that anticipated consequences are always valued exclusively in terms of personal preferences. Alternatives actions are judged in terms of the extent to which their expected future consequences are perceived to serve the preferences of the decision maker.

March (1994, pp. 2–3) efficiently summarizes his discussion of the rational model as follows:

> A rational procedure is one that pursues a logic of consequence. It makes a choice conditional on the answers to four basic questions:
> 1. The question of alternatives: What actions are possible?
> 2. The question of expectations: What future consequences might follow from each alternative? How likely is each possible consequence, assuming that an alternative is chosen?

3. The question of preferences: How valuable (to the decision maker) are the consequences associated with each of the alternatives?

4. The question of the decision rule: How is a choice to be made among the alternatives in terms of the values of the consequences?

There can be no debate that careful, systematic, and thorough attention to these four questions has improved, and will continue to improve, the efficiency of decision making. A favorite example from the literature of managerial accounting will help to clarify.

Suppose that Dan Smith, the proprietor of a small ice cream shop, has just purchased a new ice cream maker for $20,000. He expects that the machine will last ten years with no future salvage value. Maintenance and other costs to run the machine are expected to be about $1,000 per year. Smith is happy with the new machine. Its capacity is more than adequate to meet the demands of his modest clientele, and he is delighted to be rid of the old machine. Three days after the purchase, super salesman Buck Starr meets Smith at a local chamber of commerce meeting. Smith, still excited about his recent purchase, brags to Starr about it. Starr turns to Smith: "You should have talked to me first. We just found out about a new advanced ice cream maker which sells for substantially less, and is considerably more efficient in terms of annual maintenance costs." Smith learns that Starr's machine, with the same capacity as his, sells for just $8,000, and the annual cost of running the machine is only $300. The advanced ice cream maker also has an expected life of ten years, with no future salvage value.

Smith's initial exuberance over his recent purchase suddenly vanishes, but he's not about to buy a second ice cream maker in the span of just three days. (He owned his first machine for more than fifteen years.) Smith reasons, "Even if I could sell my new machine for $4,000, I can't afford a $16,000 loss this year (the original $20,000 minus the $4,000). My business is simply too small to absorb a huge blow like that."

Dan Smith would do well to reconsider. This simple scenario provides a concrete example of the benefits associated with a careful application of the rational model. At the heart of the rational model is the assertion that actions should be compared only in terms of expected future consequences. As managerial accountants often remind us, "Sunk costs are irrelevant for decision making." In the case at hand, Smith has two alternative actions. If he keeps the newly purchased machine, his total cash out will be $10,000 over the course of the next ten years. Alternatively, he can sell the newly purchased machine for $4,000 today, and turn around and buy Starr's more efficient ice cream maker for $8,000. The net cost of Starr's machine is thus only $4,000. In addition, under this alternative, Smith will incur $3,000 in maintenance costs. Total cash out under the second alternative is only $7,000. If Smith prefers more cash to less cash, the "rational" choice is obvious. Smith's reasoning that he cannot afford the huge $16,000 loss this year is spurious. The $20,000 sunk cost is irrelevant in this context. For simplicity, we assume a 0 percent interest rate. (For further discussion of related examples see Horngren and Foster 1987, chap. 9.)

This example is by no means unique. Other examples of improved decision making in business as a result of a better and more thorough application of the rational model abound. Investors interested in maximizing their returns have been served well by insights gleaned from portfolio theory. Money managers depend heavily on the concept of the time value of money. Corporate managers contemplating new investments have succeeded by applying notions of cost-benefit analysis and capital budgeting. Marketing experts have improved their techniques by applying sophisticated statistical tools. Although this list could be multiplied easily, it is really not necessary.

With such successes in mind, one might even be tempted to argue that in McCoy's ethical conflict the decision outcome could have been improved by a more self-conscious use of the rational model as outlined above. Thoroughgoing proponents of the rational decision making model would propose, perhaps, that the failure here, if indeed there is a failure, is not too much rationality, but too little.

First, McCoy did not carefully identify all the possible alternatives. An "intendedly" rational strategy requires decision makers to consider the full set of available options (March 1994). McCoy's self-report, taken at face value, suggests that at the moment of decision, he never considered the option of forgoing the climb in order to help Stephen carry the sadhu down to safety.

Second, it is clear from McCoy's description that he initially did not consider the connection between his decision to continue the climb and the ultimate well-being of the Indian holy man. McCoy was apparently taken by surprise when Stephen finally joined him at the summit. McCoy writes (p. 193),

> Still exhilarated by victory, I ran down the slope to congratulate him [Stephen]. He was suffering from altitude sickness, walking fifteen steps, then stopping, walking fifteen steps, then stopping. Pasang accompanied him all the way up. When I reached them, Stephen glared at me and said: "How do you feel about contributing to the death of a fellow man?"

The "exhilarated" McCoy was genuinely surprised by the question.

Third, and perhaps most important, preferences were not systematically examined. Throughout the ordeal, and even immediately afterward, McCoy takes it as self-evident that climbing the mountain is the "apex of one of the most powerful experiences" (p. 195) of his life. The possibility that saving the life of a desperately helpless human being—last seen lying on the ground listlessly throwing rocks at a dog—might also have proved to be an even more powerful experience was never seriously contemplated.

Proponents of the rational argument, assuming they would acknowledge that an ethical failure occurred, might want to conclude, then, that McCoy simply failed to act rationally in the strict sense that we are employing the term here. If he had been better trained as a rational decision maker, and perhaps absent the intense physical pressures of the ordeal, McCoy would have carefully contemplated the available options and realized that his own self-interest, his own real preferences, dictated abandoning the climb and saving the sadhu. Proponents of the rational argument might argue that he really preferred saving the man's life but was not consciously aware of this at the moment of decision. If this diagnosis is correct, the solution is more rationality, not less. Conceding the importance of this argument (there is a kernel of truth here), the final conclusion is dubious. A more plausible interpretation of McCoy's report suggests that at the very moment of decision, he was indeed acting rationally, if by acting rationally we merely mean that he was promoting his own perceived interests—as he perceived them at that moment. He might very well have considered all his options and their possible ramifications. Nevertheless, at the moment of decision, McCoy's preference for reaching the summit overwhelmed his desire to help the sadhu. The immediate prospect of successfully achieving a long-sought goal simply dwarfed the perceived personal benefits associated with the uncertain prospect of saving the sadhu.

Most of us, with a little self-reflection, can call to mind incidents where we pursued some activity that provided momentary satisfaction, but that we "knew," even at the decisive moment, was not the "correct" course of action. Psychologists have noted that there is a tendency for immediate rewards to appear misleadingly attractive. Immediate rewards flood one's conscience and overwhelm one's judgments. This problem has been called the weak will problem. Robert Frank (1988, p. 80) expands:

> When a pigeon is given a chance to peck one of two buttons to choose between a morsel of food 30 seconds from now and a much larger morsel 40 seconds from now, it takes the latter. But when it chooses between the same morsel now and the larger morsel 10 seconds hence, it often picks the former. Rats behave the same way. So do cats, dogs,

guinea pigs, and hogs. And so, much of the time, do humans. This feature is apparently part of the hard-wiring of most animal nervous systems.

Individuals with dangerously high levels of cholesterol know that eating foods high in saturated fats will increase their risk of a heart attack, yet they continue to consume red meats and cheeses. All of us are aware of the risks associated with cigarettes, yet smoking persists. In business, creators of Ponzi schemes surely must know that ultimately the strategy is self-defeating, yet in the excitement of discovery, the lure of magnificent gains often make Ponzi schemes too difficult to resist. It is interesting to speculate that the problem of the weak will may have its analogue at the level of the organization. If this speculation holds, it obviously has important implications for business ethics. Both for-profit and not-for-profit organizations often endorse, support, and, most importantly, reward activities that promote perceived short-term goals. These same activities, however, ultimately work against the long-term interests of the organization. In some cases, the pursuit and attainment of short-term goals can even lead to the extinction of the enterprise.

In the heat of the moment, for example, the immediate rewards of increased short-term profitability are perceived by organizational leaders as irresistible. At some level, it makes sense to say that top management "knows" that the pursuit of short-term goals is wrong, but the felt pressures of shareholders and competitors make it impossible to adjust behavior accordingly. In the not-for-profit sector, a university or college might find it difficult to avoid a strategy of diluting academic standards in favor of increasing student enrollment. Administrators and faculty may even be aware that the plan is ultimately self-defeating. It is surely not difficult to predict that as students, graduate schools, and prospective employers learn that academic quality has deteriorated, students will quickly adapt their behavior and seek other institutions. Nevertheless, the ability to increase student enrollment today may prove too tempting for some universities to resist. Institutions exhibit behavior similar to the dieter who desires just one more piece of Bavarian chocolate cake even when she knows well the health risks associated with obesity.

Similarly, one wonders how a 232-year-old British investment bank, with impeccable credentials and a hard-won reputation as a bastion of conservative investing, could have allowed a twenty-something yuppie the freedom to wager (and ultimately lose) more than a billion dollars worth of capital. In the span of about five years, the British investment bank, Baring's, promoted Nicholas Leeson from a back-office clerk, responsible for making sure that transactions were properly accounted for, to chief trader at the bank's Singapore operation. Further, Baring's granted Leeson a rare degree of autonomy. He was in the unusual position of being chief trader and responsible for settling all his trades. These roles are usually separated to lessen the likelihood of rogue trading. Leeson was able to maintain his dual responsibility in spite of the fact that there were warnings. There is now evidence that other traders were cautioning that Leeson was a "gunslinger." Further, and more importantly, as early as March 1992, an internal fax warned that "we are in danger of setting up a structure which will prove disastrous, in which we would succeed in losing either a lot of money, client goodwill or both" (*Time,* March 13, 1995).

With these warnings in mind, it is even more difficult to understand how such a colossal failure happens. An internal audit, dated from August 1994, provides a clue. Despite the risks of allowing Leeson to continue trading huge amounts of capital with little or no supervision, the audit, obtained by the *Financial Times,* recommended that although Leeson was a risk, his departure would "speed the erosion of Baring's Futures' profitability. . . . Without him, Baring's Futures' would lack a trader with the right combination of experience, contacts, trading skills, and local knowledge." A possible explanation, then, is that it was simply too difficult for the organization to forgo the huge short-term profits. It was thought, at the time, that Leeson had brought in between $20 million and $36 million for Baring's during 1994. The irresistible attraction of this kind of money prevented Baring's, as an organization, from carefully investigating the nature of these profits. In other words, Baring's was trapped by the lure of enormous short-term gains, even while top management knew that a problem existed.

The view propounded here suggests that technically speaking, at the moment of decision, each of the "failures" discussed above, both at the level of the individual and at the level of the organization, reflects behavior consistent with canons of rationality; i.e., in each case, decision makers were promoting perceived self-interest. As Frank further notes, "Given the nature of our psychological reward mechanism, a person who is purely self-interested will sometimes give in to his temptation to cheat, even when he knows cheating does not pay" (p. 88). (For a different interpretation, see Nozick 1993, pp. 14–21.)

The Logic of Appropriateness

The problem that Frank and others (Ainslie 1985, Elster 1985) have identified is that our preferences are often structured such that the prospect of immediate gratification overwhelms our more permanent long-run interests. Somewhat paradoxically, one solution to the weak will problem is to abandon self-interest in favor of an alternative vision of human behavior. It is paradoxical because abandoning pure rationality often promotes long-run interests. James March has labeled this alternative vision the logic of appropriateness. According to March (p. 58), the logic of appropriateness, like the rational model, can be summarized by a set of questions.

> Decision makers are imagined to ask (explicitly or implicitly) three questions:
>
> 1. The question of recognition: What kind of situation is this?
>
> 2. The question of identity. What kind of a person am I? Or what kind of organization is this?

3. The question of rules: What does a person such as I, or an organization such as this, do in a situation such as this?

The essence of the logic of appropriateness is the notion that decision making is ultimately not about promoting one's immediate self-interest, and is better envisaged as understanding, interpreting, and accepting ethical principles or rules of behavior. This perspective asserts that it is meaningful to talk about behavior as if behavior is meaningful (independent of personal preferences). As March himself makes explicit, "Decision makers can violate a logic of consequence and be considered stupid or naive, but if they violate the moral obligations of identity, they will be considered lacking in elementary virtue" (p. 65).

To be sure, a logic of appropriateness recognizes that some behavior is dictated by individual self-interest, but the domain where self-interest commands jurisdiction is ultimately bounded by rules of appropriateness. Arthur Okun (1975), for example, carefully describes what he terms "the domain of rights" (p. 6). (Walzer 1983, p. 97, uses the term "blocked exchanges" to describe the same phenomenon.) Okun emphasizes that democratic societies like the United States "bestow upon us the right to obtain equal justice, to exercise freedom of speech and religion, to vote, to take a spouse and procreate, to be free in our persons in the sense of immunity from enslavement, to disassociate ourselves from American society by emigration, as well as various claims on public services such as police protection and public education" (p. 6). One of the important features of rights (and obligations) is the fact that they cannot be bought or sold in the market. Okun elaborates (pp. 9–10):

> It takes only a little imagination to envision many new markets in rights that might arise if trades were permitted. The ban on indentured service is an obviously coercive limitation on free trade; it discourages investments by businessmen in the training and skills of their employees, and prevents bargains that might be beneficial to both the seller

of his person and the buyer. The one-person, one-spouse rule could be altered to permit voluntary exchange by giving each person a marketable ticket to a spouse rather than a non-transferable right to marry one (and no more than one) person at a time. Since jury trials are expensive, society might offer any defendant who waived that right some portion of the savings. Trade in military draft obligations is easy to conceive and, in fact, has occurred in the past. Even the obligation to obey the law might be made marketable, as it was, in a figurative sense, when the Church sold indulgences during the Middle Ages.

Okun provocatively asks what can possibly justify these infringements on liberty. If indeed one can envision and point to societies where these rights are exchanged in the marketplace, why do democratic societies tolerate such limitations on the pursuit of individual self-interest?

Okun suggests that one reason society enforces rights is that a viable society has "to rest on a broad base of human motives and human interests" (p. 12). Self-interest is only one of the motives for human behavior. The existence of human rights helps to prevent the economic realm from dominating and subordinating all of our relationships. Okun's point, in part, seems to be that rights (and obligations) serve an important symbolic function. By clearly demarcating the domain of rights, society reminds itself that not everything can be translated into economic terms. "The domain of rights is part of the checks and balances on the market designed to preserve values that are not denominated in dollars" (p. 13). Or, as the Bible puts it, "Man does not live by bread alone" (Deuteronomy 8:3).

Okun's view, consistent with the biblical vision, is that the rational model, understood as *the* model of human behavior, is myopic. It describes only part of the deeply felt reality of human decision making. As Amitai Etzioni (1988) has perceptively noted, "The neoclassical paradigm (the rational model) is too simple: it does not include a pivotal distinction between the sense of pleasure—derived from consumption of goods and services, and from other sources—and the sense of affirmation attained when a person abides by his or her moral commitments" (p. 36). Further, Etzioni asserts that casual empirical observation "shows that individuals who seek to live up to their moral commitments behave in a manner that is systematically and significantly different from those who act to enhance their pleasures" (p. 67).

The paradoxical benefit of principled behavior is that it can serve as a mechanism for avoiding the weak will problem. For example, a diligent and honest business person, tempted by the prospects of the immediate gains of a Ponzi scheme, might do well to recall, at the moment of decision, the principle that one is entitled to a profit only after producing a product or service with social value. With the aid of a deeply held principle, even the most narrowly self-interested calculus might now call for forgoing the Ponzi scheme. The principled business person might reason as follows. "Although I attach a very high preference to immediate material rewards like money, the equally immediate sense of accomplishment (or affirmation) I will feel as a result of honoring my principle, coupled with the expected guilt I will feel if I break my principle, is more than sufficient to prevent me from participating in the Ponzi scheme." Careful notice and special emphasis should be given to the fact that the principle must be accepted for its own sake (i.e., it must give rise to true feelings of accomplishment or guilt), and cannot simply be invoked as a "trick" to avoid temptation. This insight is captured in the Jewish tradition in the very first chapter of the Ethics of the Fathers:

> Antigonus of Sokho received the oral tradition from Simeon the Just. He used to say: "Be not like servants who serve the master for the sake of receiving a reward, but be like servants who serve the master without the expectation of receiving a reward; and let the fear of Heaven be upon you."

Perhaps the real decision McCoy and his fellow hikers faced was not how best to promote their own self-interest, but whether or not the rational model was *appropriate* as the dominant mode of decision making. In other words, McCoy failed because he viewed his decision purely in terms of self-interest. The decision was framed as simply one more opportunity to promote individual preferences. Had McCoy chosen an alternative frame—what we are calling a logic of appropriateness—the decision outcome might have been improved.

To some readers, it may seem strange to suggest, as is being done here, that decision making can be influenced simply by altering the formulation of the problem. Nevertheless, the psychologists Amos Tversky and Daniel Kahneman (1981) have adroitly demonstrated that "preference reversals" of exactly this form can easily be elicited from experimental subjects. They write (p. 453):

> It is often possible to frame a given decision problem in more than one way. Alternative frames for a decision problem may be compared to alternative perspectives on a visual scene. Veridical perception requires that the perceived relative heights of two neighboring mountains, say, should not reverse with changes of vantage point. Similarly, rational choice requires that the preference between options should not reverse with changes of frame. Because of imperfections of human perception and decision, however, changes of perspective often reverse the relative apparent size of objects and the relative desirability of options.

The most dramatic framing effect reported by Tversky and Kahneman report occurred in response to two versions of the following scenario, where respondents were asked to choose between hypothetical options. The first version read (p. 453):

> Imagine that the U.S. is preparing for the outbreak of an unusual Asian disease, which is expected to kill 600 people. Two alternative programs to combat the disease have been proposed. Assume that the exact scientific estimate of the consequences of the programs are as follows:

If Program A is adopted, 200 people will be saved.

If Program B is adopted, there is 1/3 probability that 600 people will be saved, and 2/3 probability that no people will be saved.

A strong majority of respondents (72 percent) chose the "less risky" option, Program A. The expectation of certainly saving 200 lives is viewed as superior to the risky option of saving all 600 people. This result, in and of itself, is not unusual. However, a second set of respondents, when given the same cover story but with a different formulation of the options, responded exactly opposite. The second set of options was expressed as follows (p. 453):

If Program C is adopted 400 people will die.

If Program D is adopted there is 1/3 probability that nobody will die, and 2/3 probability that 600 people will die.

Here, only 22 percent chose Program C, and 78 percent preferred Program D, a pattern reflecting a preference for risk taking, even though Programs A and C, and B and D are functionally equivalent. Tversky and Kahneman's robust finding has important implications. They conclude their paper by underscoring (p. 458),

The framing of acts and outcomes can also reflect the acceptance or rejection of responsibility for particular consequences, and the deliberate manipulation of framing is commonly used as an instrument of self-control. *When framing influences the experience of consequences, the adoption of a decision frame is an ethically significant act* [emphasis added].

Let us suppose that McCoy had taken the "ethically significant act" of framing his choice in terms of the logic of appropriateness. Unlike the angry New Zealander, who peremptorily

turned and went back up the mountain to join his friends, McCoy
would have stepped outside of himself and asked March's first
question, "What kind of a situation is this?" Arguably, in this
instance, the mere asking of the question would have been sufficient. Had McCoy been able to admit to himself, at the moment
of decision, that continuing the climb would contribute (even
indirectly) to the death of the sadhu, it is highly unlikely that he
would have chosen as he did. Stephen's question to McCoy is
pertinent in this context. At the summit, he asks the following
rhetorical question: "I wonder what the Sherpas would have
done if the sadhu had been a well-dressed Nepali, or what the
Japanese would have done if the sadhu had been a well-dressed
Asian, or what you would have done, Buzz, if the sadhu had been
a well-dressed Western woman?" (p. 195). Stephen's question
drives home the point that a human being's life was hanging in
the balance. In the dilemma described here, nationality, wealth,
and mode of dress are obviously not relevant factors. Being able
to see through these externals, even in the heat of the moment, is
an important first step in describing and resolving true ethical
dilemmas.

Important as March's first question is, the second and third
questions reflect the essence of the logic of appropriateness and
distinguish it as an alternative mode of decision making. "What
kind of a person am I?" This question subsumes the question of
preferences which is at the foundation of the rational model.
Here, however, not only does one ask how a given action will
promote current preferences, but one is enjoined to question
those very preferences. This question and March's third question,
"What does a person such as I, or an organization such as this, do
in a situation such as this?", invite and encourage the decision
maker to utilize ethical and/or religious criteria. The ability to
critique one's own preferences (assumed in the second question)
and alter them (assumed in the third question) are the heart and
soul of the logic of appropriateness. Herein lies the major distinction between a purely rational model and the logic of appropriateness.

By contrast, the rational model always take preferences as completely stable and exogenous. "Preferences are assumed not to change substantially over time, not to be very different between wealthy and poor persons, or even between persons in different societies and cultures" (Becker 1976, p. 5; see also Stigler and Becker 1977). The assumption underlying this view is that tastes will be unchanged even when the outcomes of actions taken today are realized (March 1978). Further, standard theories of choice assume that tastes are absolute. "Normative theories of choice assume a formal posture of moral relativism. The theories insist on morality of action in terms of tastes; but they recognize neither discriminations among alternative tastes, nor the possibility that a person reasonably might view his own preferences and actions based on them as morally distressing" (March 1978, p. 595). Advocates of the rational model ignore the effects of education, art, literature, community, religious beliefs, persuasion, and the role of leadership. Etzioni (1988, p. 10) criticizes this view. He writes it is "as if economic man was a biological-psychological miracle born fully formed, say in his mid-twenties with his preferences `immaculately conceived' as Kenneth Boulding put it to a 1985 George Washington University Seminar on socio-economics." After the fact, commenting on his own behavior, McCoy himself seemingly recognizes the failure of the rational model, and in turn his own personal failure in this instance. The tremendous depth and power of "The Parable of the Sadhu" derives in large measure from McCoy's vulnerable, honest, and perceptive self-criticism, which ultimately lead him to embrace a logic of appropriateness (p. 199):

> What would have happened had Stephen and I carried the sadhu for two days back to the village and become involved with the villagers in his care? In four trips to Nepal my most interesting experiences occurred in 1975 when I lived in a Sherpa home in the Khumbu for five days recovering from altitude sickness. The high point of Stephen's trip was an invitation to participate in a family funeral ceremony

in Manang. Neither experience had to do with climbing the
high passes of the Himalayas. Why were we so reluctant to
try the lower path, the ambiguous trail?

McCoy's final conclusion is unintelligible from a purely rational approach. His language is the language of appropriateness
rather than self-interest. Focusing specifically on business ethics,
he anticipates March's second and third questions when he finally concludes his essay, "What is the nature of our responsibility if we consider ourselves to be ethical persons? Perhaps it is to
change the values of the group so that it can, with all its resources,
take the other road" (p. 200).

How "Realistic" Is A Logic of Appropriateness?

For those, like McCoy, engaged in "challenging the egoistic
paradigm" (Bowie 1991), there are reasons for optimism. Kenneth
E. Goodpaster (1991, p. 89), a leading spokesperson for business
ethics, describes the following recent developments:

> 1. Business schools are reaching both outward and in-
> ward to address the moral dimensions of their educational
> mission.
> 2. Students of business are demonstrating increasing con-
> cern about ethical values as they prepare for professional
> business careers.
> 3. Corporate leaders and executives are reflecting more
> than ever before on the ethical aspects of business life.
> 4. Philosophers and other scholars in the humanities are
> widening their commitment to constructive social and insti-
> tutional criticism.
> 5. The media are expanding the public's understanding
> of both the conceptual and practical implications of ethical
> criticism.

The logic of appropriateness has a certain rhetorical appeal. It
is certainly consistent with what many of us would like to believe

about human nature. But in spite of the important individual and institutional changes documented by Goodpaster, there remains a nagging skepticism which must be addressed. Is a logic of appropriateness realistic? This skepticism is usually reflected through two specific and related questions. First, skeptics wonder, if the logic of appropriateness is taken to be a valid description of how people actually behave, is there any evidence that supports it? Skeptics want more than a description of isolated heroic instances of soldiers sacrificing their lives by jumping on live grenades, or mothers willingly giving up their own lives to save the lives of their children. Second, even if one were to demonstrate the existence of widespread ethical behavior, can ethical behavior persist over long periods of time? In other words, assuming that an individual or a business enterprise framed decisions along the lines advocated here, could this action be sustained over the long run? The second question implicitly suggests that ethical behavior is self-defeating. Both of these questions deserve attention.

Does Anyone Really Accept the Self-Interest Model?

Imagine the following situation. You are recruited to participate in a laboratory experiment. The experimenter tells you he will give you $20, with the stipulation that you must divide the cash with a second participant in the experiment. The instructions explain that you can allocate the $20 *however you choose.* Once you have made up your mind, your proposal is submitted to the second participant. There is absolutely no communication between the two of you. If he or she accepts your offer, you each receive the agreed-upon share of the $20, and the experiment is over. If the second participant rejects the offer, neither of you receives any cash, and again the experiment is over. Both of you are aware that the experiment is played once, and only once. You do not know the second participant's identity, nor does the second participant know your identity. Further, the experimenter guarantees that neither participant will ever learn the other participant's identity. Carefully consider how you would allocate the money.

True believers in the self-interest model have only one real choice here. If you accept the assumptions of the self-interest model as a description not only of your own behavior but as a description of all human behavior (if only in the economic sphere), the only rational allocation is to offer one penny to the second participant and take the remaining $19.99 for oneself. This conclusion holds because the goal of the solely self-interested player is to extract as much cash as possible from the experiment. Further, under the belief that both participants are solely self-interested, the goal of the second participant must also be to extract as much cash as possible from the experiment. A clever self-interested participant quickly notices that it is never in the self-interest of the second participant to reject any positive proposal, no matter how small. Even under the most lopsided proposal, the first participant, being a true believer in the self-interest model, knows that the second participant must prefer some cash to no cash. The true believer must reason that the second participant will never choose to "punish" him for an "unfair" proposal, because such behavior would be contrary to the second participant's own self-interest. The second participant gains nothing from rejecting the offer. (This, of course, would not be true if the second participant thought there might be additional rounds of the experiment. In a multi-period setting, "punishing" the first player might lead to more equal proposals in later stages of the game. Thus the strategy of forgoing a small reward in an early round might lead to long-term gains.)

Actual empirical results, as reported by Guth, Schmittberger, and Schwarze (1982), suggest that most of us are not true believers in the self-interest model. The results indicate that the vast majority of respondents do not propose a one-sided allocation. The most common proposal, in the fifty-one independent trials conducted, was a fifty-fifty split. Importantly, in those few cases (six of fifty-one trials) where an extremely uneven proposal was made, the second participant refused the offer (five of six trials). The behavior reported here is clearly inconsistent with the pure model of self-interest. Rather, participants demonstrate behavior much more compatible with the logic of appropriateness. They reason and act as if they believe that norms of fairness exist and matter (Bowie 1991).

Additional Evidence That Ethics Matters

Amitai Etzioni (1988, pp. 51–66) has catalogued numerous studies that document unselfish behavior. Some of the evidence he cites is briefly summarized below:

> 1. People will mail back lost wallets to complete strangers, even at positive costs to themselves (Hornstein, Fisch, and Holmes 1968).
> 2. A high proportion of people who are approached for help by strangers choose to assist those in distress (Latane and Darley, 1970).
> 3. Numerous experiments, under different conditions, show that subjects do not take free rides, but voluntarily pay as much as 40 to 60 percent of what economists calculate would be due the public till if the subject did not free ride (Marwell and Ames 1981).
> 4. Individuals vote even when there is little or no chance that their votes can impact the outcome of the election. Party affiliation and ideology had strong effects, while self-interest had almost no effect (Sears et al. 1980, p. 679).

The details of these studies are less important than their cumulative impact. The main reason for introducing this material here is simply to document the ample and overwhelming evidence that people can and do act unselfishly. Perhaps to non-economists it may seem quite strange to prove the existence of behavior that most of us, most of the time, take as self-evident. Why prove the obvious? (Etzioni 1988) The truth is, however, that many economists, as well as other social scientists influenced by the economists' assumptions, spend much of their working lives trying to explain all human behavior as a direct result of self-interested motives. Economists instinctively reject explanations that invoke the language of morality. Thus the studies briefly described above become important.

The Sustainability of Ethical Behavior

The discussion in this section begins with two assumptions. First, assume for the moment that the demands of a logic of appropriateness require, from time to time, true acts of "hardcore" altruism. Here, we are not talking about a "gift" given today with the unstated but implicit condition that it will be reciprocated in the future. Rather, hardcore altruism requires that agents initiate actions where no future material benefits are expected. In fact, agents engaging in hardcore altruism willingly incur individual costs in order to undertake the acts. Illustrative examples might include an individual who anonymously donates blood to strangers out of a perceived sense of social responsibility, or someone who jumps into a freezing river to save a drowning child because of a felt moral obligation. The ultimate act of altruism is to surrender one's life out of a sense of duty. Judaism, for example, demands that one willingly give up one's life rather than engage in idolatry, sexual immorality, or murder. Hardcore altruism, however, need not entail such heroic acts. It may exist whenever an individual has an opportunity to promote individual interests but refrains from doing so out of a perceived sense of duty. Second, let us assume, following the discussion above, that such behavior actually exists even in the realm of economic behavior. In other words, we assume that a significant proportion of the population will periodically, but reliably, choose behavior which is not motivated out of a desire to promote their own or even close relatives' preferences; i.e., they will perform acts of hardcore altruism.

Under these two assumptions an important but simple question emerges. Wouldn't the altruists, who by definition engage in activities detrimental to their own material well-being, eventually lose out to the purely self-interested? Over long periods of time, individuals or groups that pass on an ethical tradition (through either a genetic predisposition, a cultural heritage, or some combination of both) would eventually and inevitably become completed dominated by individuals or groups that relentlessly pursue their own material well-being. Even if we could imagine individuals who engage in altruism, and even if the altruists contribute more than their share to the communal welfare as a whole, ultimately altruistic acts are self-defeating. The self-interested may enjoy the benefits conferred upon them by the altruists, but the self-interested are too clever to join in. As long as there is even a small remnant of self-interested individuals, evolutionary forces will dictate that there is nothing the altruists can do. (A parallel argument is often made at the level of the business organization. Here, market forces replace evolutionary forces as the "natural" mechanism that ensures the survival of the fittest.)

This view suggests that ethics is merely an additional constraint on the feasible set of available actions. The self-interested, if it is in their self-interest, can, at worst, always willingly choose to restrict their behavior to mimic the altruistic. The self-interested, therefore, might present themselves in public as altruists. Thus they always do at least as well as the altruists. However, the self-interested have the flexibility of abandoning duty or principle whenever there exists an opportunity for individual gain. If they have an opportunity to secretly cheat, they always will. Therefore, not only do the self-interested do at least as well as the altruists, but they can consistently beat the altruists, who are bound to forgo precisely these kinds of opportunities.

Robert H. Frank (1988), in *Passions Within Reason*, has carefully attacked and defeated this argument. His view has very important implications for those advocating the possibility of a logic of appropriateness as an alternative to pure models of rationality. Frank suggests that human beings are often faced with what he calls commitment problems. He suggests that commitment problems arise when it is in one's interest to make a binding pledge today to behave in ways that will go against one's self-interest tomorrow. The following example (pp. 47–48) is typical:

Two persons, Smith and Jones, can engage in a potentially profitable venture, say, a restaurant. Their potential for gain arises from the natural advantages inherent in the division and specialization of labor. Smith is a talented cook, but is shy and an incompetent manager. Jones, by contrast, cannot boil an egg, but is charming and has shrewd business judgment. Together, they have the necessary skills to launch a successful venture. Working alone, however, their potential is more limited.

Their problem is this: Each will have opportunities to cheat without possibility of detection. Jones can skim from the cash drawer without Smith's knowledge. Smith, for his part, can take kickbacks from food suppliers.

If only one of them cheats, he does very well. The non-cheater does poorly, but isn't sure why. His low return is not a reliable sign of having been cheated, since there are many benign explanations why a business might do poorly. If the victim also cheats, he, too, can escape detection, and will do better than by not cheating, but still not nearly as well as if both had been honest.

Once the venture is under way, self-interest unambiguously dictates cheating. Yet if both could make a binding commitment not to cheat, they would profit by doing so.

Such commitment problems are quite commonplace. Frank provides numerous additional examples related to military deterrence, economic bargaining, and even marriage.

Frank further suggests that the essential characteristics of the commitment problem can be captured parsimoniously through the use of a familiar model in the social sciences, the prisoners' dilemma. A version of the prisoners' dilemma sufficient for the present purposes can be summarized as follows. Suppose you and an associate are considering a new joint project. Each of you has two, and only two, options. You can choose either to cooperate or to defect. If both parties choose to cooperate, the monetary payoff from the project will be $4,000 each. If both parties choose to defect, the monetary payoff is significantly reduced to only $2,000 each. However, if one of you chooses to cooperate, while the other chooses to defect, the defecter gains while the cooperator loses. In this case, the defecter will receive $6,000 and the cooperator gets $0. The payoffs are summarized in the following table.

Prisoners' Dilemma — Outcomes

	Player 1 Cooperates		Player 1 Defects	
Player 2 Cooperates	$4,000	(P1)	$6,000	(P1)
	$4,000	(P2)	$0	(P2)
Player 2 Defects	$0	(P1)	$2,000	(P1)
	$6,000	(P2)	$2,000	(P2)

This table summarizes the outcomes of the prisoners' dilemma.

The dilemma in the prisoners' dilemma is this. If the nature of the project is such that it is a onetime opportunity, strategies based on pure self-interest always lead to the inferior $2,000 payoff rather than the available $4,000 payoff. This is true because both participants reason as follows. "Regardless of what my associate chooses, I am always better off defecting rather than cooperating. If the other person chooses to cooperate, by defecting I increase my payoff from $4,000 to $6,000. On the other hand, if the other person chooses to defect, by defecting I increase my payoff from $0 to $2,000. Therefore, defecting dominates, and I always choose to defect." Since both participants reason the same way, the payoff is always $2,000 each, even where $4,000 was seemingly within reach.

Note that this somewhat unfortunate result holds even if the two of you can openly discuss the strategy in advance. Suppose, for example, that you are allowed ample opportunity to discuss the prisoners' dilemma with each other before making your choices. Once you have finished the discussion, however, your actual choices are still made in private. Given the structure of the payoffs, in a few moments of discussion you would probably both come to realize that it is in your mutual interest to cooperate. The two of you might even verbally commit to cooperate. But from the standpoint of pure self-interest, nothing has changed at the moment of decision, because the payoffs are still the same. Thus the person who defects is still always better off. As long as both of you remain committed to the pure model of rationality, there is no chance of gaining the elusive $4,000 prize.

Frank uses the structure of the prisoners' dilemma to demonstrate how altruism can be sustained over long periods of time. The altruist, recall, is an individual who has an opportunity to promote individual interests but refrains from doing so out of a perceived sense of duty. At first blush, it might seem that altruists would fare quite poorly in a world full of prisoners' dilemmas. If an altruist faced off against a self-interested player, the altruist would abide by his prior commitment and would receive $0, while the self-interested person would casually ignore his commitment, choose to defect, and receive $6,000. "Cooperators, even if they make up almost the entire population to begin with, are thus destined for extinction" (p. 59).

Frank emphasizes, however, that if altruists could recognize one another, they would do quite well. Suppose altruists and the self-interested were easily identifiable. In this world, altruists would always seek out other altruists. If two altruists committed to the cooperative strategy, their private choices would reflect their commitments. Two altruists would therefore receive $4,000 each and beat two self-interested players, who would receive only $2,000 each. In fact, if one's reputation for altruism or self-interest always reflected one's true character, altruistic behavior would eventually come to dominate. Frank suggests. in evolutionary terms, that "the cooperators' larger payoffs enable *them* to raise larger families, which means they will make up an ever-growing share of the population. When cooperators can be easily identified, it is the defectors who face extinction" (pp. 59–60). While this result is interesting, it accomplishes too much. Not only do altruists do quite well, they take over completely. In this version of the model, there is no room for self-interest at all.

To avoid this problem, Frank introduces an additional but realistic assumption. He suggests that in the real world, there may be a cost to determining whether someone is an altruist or not. Extending the current example, suppose that for a $1,000 fee ("inspection cost") one can always distinguish between the altruists and the self-interested. Would an altruist be willing to pay the fee? An altruist who pays the $1,000 fee will always choose to interact with another altruist, and therefore will receive a net payoff of $3,000. On the other hand, an altruist who chooses not to pay the fee will randomly interact with either an altruist or a self-interested person. If he has the good fortune of selecting another altruist, he will receive $4,000, but if the chosen partner is self-interested, the altruist gets nothing. If one does not pay the fee, the expected payoff is dependent on the makeup of the population.

Is it worthwhile for the altruist to pay the fee? It depends. Under the assumptions we have been making, if more than 75 percent of the population are altruists, it would not make sense to pay the fee. For example, suppose 90 percent of the population are altruists. An altruist who chooses not to pay the $1,000 fee will, on average, receive $3,600 (0.90 x $4,000 + 0.10 x $0). This beats the $3,000 he would get if he chooses to pay the fee. If less than 75 percent of the population are altruists, it is better to pay the fee. Suppose 50 percent of the population are altruists. Here, an altruist who chooses not to pay the fee will, on average, receive only $2,000 (0.50 x $4,000 + .050 x $0). In this case, paying the fee is the better choice.

In the light of the preceding analysis, it is clear that the population will stabilize at 75 percent altruists and 25 percent self-interested. If altruists make up more than 75 percent of the population, the self-interested do better than the altruists and the percentage of self-interested is expected to grow. The expected return for the self-interested when the mix is 90 percent altruists is \$5,600 (0.90 x \$6,000 + 0.10 x \$2,000). By contrast, if altruists make up less than 75 percent of the population, the altruists do better than the self-interested. The expected return for the self-interested when the mix is 50 percent altruists is just \$2,000. Recall that at this mix, all the altruists pay the \$1,000 fee to avoid the self-interested.

Obviously, the 75 percent equilibrium is merely a function of the arbitrary assumptions invoked here to generate the discussion. There is nothing special about the 75 percent equilibrium. Rather, the importance of the exercise, as Frank explains, is to demonstrate that "when there are costs of scrutiny, there will be pressures that pull the population toward some stable mix of cooperators and defectors. . . . This result stands in stark contrast to the traditional sociobiological result that only opportunism can survive" (p. 63). In addition, this version of the model avoids the awkward result that no opportunism can survive.

To summarize, in Frank's view the key to understanding how altruism can be sustained is the idea that reputation matters. In a world where reputations are meaningless, the self-interested come to dominate. In a world where reputations are completely accurate and freely available, altruists come to dominate. However, in a world where reputations are accurate, but are available only after the inspection fee is paid, both altruism and self-interest can survive. Frank's view suggests that ethics should not be viewed merely as an additional constraint on the feasible set of available actions. Ethics serves a positive role in helping to solve the ubiquitous commitment problem.

This section began with two assumptions. First, we assumed that the demands of a logic of appropriateness periodically require true acts of hardcore altruism. Second, we assumed that altruism exists. The conclusion of this discussion is that altruism is not self-defeating. In fact, there is strong reason to believe that under appropriately specified conditions altruism can persist and flourish. This conclusion is a necessary starting point for any kind of advocacy of the logic of appropriateness.

The Religious Point of View

Proponents of the rational model believe that ultimately the model of appropriateness can be folded back into the rational model. They do not deny ethics outright, but suggest that ultimately self-interest explains the existence of ethical principles. In other words, self-interest is the independent variable, and ethics is the dependent variable. In this sense, the rational model subsumes the model of appropriateness. It is readily acknowledged that ethics, and even a religiously grounded ethics, promotes material benefits. The following observation is not unusual: "Truth, trust, acceptance, restraint, obligation—these are among the social virtues grounded in religious belief which are also now seen to play a central role in the functioning of an individualistic, contractual economy" (Hirsch 1976, p. 141).

It may even be admitted that the maximum material benefits only accrue to those who internalize the logic of appropriateness. Even so, advocates of this position continue to insist that it makes sense to speak of ethics as being motivated by pure self-interest. This view has been given its clearest modern articulation by the economist George Akerlof (1983). Akerlof imagines a world where employers will pay honest employees more than dishonest employees. Honest employees are expected not to embezzle, and therefore employers can afford to pay them a higher salary. In such a world, parents will choose to make their children honest if, and only if, the cost of doing so is sufficiently small. In this way, parents ensure the economic well-being of their offspring. "According to the model here, it pays persons to bond themselves by acquiring traits that cause them to appear honest. And the cheapest way to acquire such traits according to our model is, in fact, to be honest!" (p. 56)

In Akerlof's world, it makes sense to think of human beings as choosing values solely for the purpose of promoting long-run material interests. In his words (p. 54):

> Most persons attempt to choose values for their children (and perhaps also for themselves) according to their eco-

nomic opportunities that allow them to get along economically. . . . not only the wealthy . . . but also the poorest of the
poor—immigrants, sharecroppers, and mountaineers—consciously teach their children values aimed at leading them
best to survive economically.

According to Akerlof, it is not simply that ethical principles
are consistent with the promotion of material well-being (the
view discussed in the preceding section), but that the acceptance
of ethical principles is always motivated by self-interest. The
model suggests that individual decision makers choose to purchase ethics as a result of exactly the same process that explains
why consumers choose to buy, say, potatoes for tonight's dinner.
Ethics is just one more commodity.

Akerlof (p. 57) maintains that while it is possible for honesty
to become a goal pursued for its own sake, such behavior is
dysfunctional.

> In my model of childrearing, honesty may begin as a
> means for economic betterment, but then there is a displace-
> ment of goals so that the person so trained will refrain from
> embezzlement where there is no penalty. Psychological ex-
> periments with animals show similarly that animals may
> quite easily be trained to have dysfunctional behavior.

Akerlof implicitly suggests that it were possible to teach one's
children to feign honesty at a low cost, most parents would
choose to do so.

It is precisely here that religiously grounded views contrast
sharply with the self-interest model. From a religious perspective,
ethics may be consistent with the rational model but cannot, in the
final analysis, be fully explained by it. Although leading an ethical
life often promotes one's material interests, one does not choose
to be ethical out of self-interest. Rather the choice is ultimately
made in an attempt to understand life as meaningful beyond the
satisfaction of material comforts. In answering March's questions

(1994, p. 58), "What kind of a person am I?" and "What does a person such as I . . . do in a situation such as this?", one must find a place for one's own preferences, but one must also be able to critique and alter those very same preferences. It is beyond dispute that from the Jewish perspective, the acceptance of ethical principles by the individual or the community is ideally not motivated by the calculus of material self-interest. Abraham Joshua Heschel (1951, p. 96) makes this point as follows:

> The most precious thing that has ever been on earth were the Two Tablets of stone which Moses received upon Mount Sinai; they were priceless beyond compare. He had gone up into the Mount to receive them; there he abode forty days and forty nights; he did neither eat bread nor drink water. And the Lord delivered unto him the Two Tablets of stone, and on them were written the Ten Commandments, the words which the Lord spoke with the people of Israel in the Mount out of the midst of fire. But when coming down the Mount at the end of forty days and forty nights—the Two Tablets in his hands—Moses saw the people dance around the Golden Calf, he cast the Tablets out of his hands and broke them before their eyes.

According to Heschel, even the "most precious thing" in the world, the tablets of stone containing God's own writing, is ephemeral. The law itself takes precedence.

Religious views begin with the model of appropriateness as axiomatic, and hold that rationality is derivative.

An important and fundamental articulation of this is the following rabbinic midrash (Lauterbach 1961, vol. 2, pp. 234–235), in which God, before giving the Torah to Israel, approaches every tribe and nation.

> He appeared to the children of Esau the wicked and said to them: Will you accept the Torah? They said to Him: What is written in it? He said to them: "Thou shalt not murder."

They said to Him: The very heritage which our father left us was: "And by thy sword shalt thou live." He then appeared to the children of Amon and Moab. He said to them: Will you accept the Torah? They said to Him: What is written in it? He said to them: "Thou shalt not commit adultery." They, however, said to Him that they were all of them children of adulterers, as it is said: "Thus were both the daughters of Lot with child by their father." Then He appeared to the children of Ishmael. He said to them: Will you accept the Torah? They said to Him: What is written in it? He said to them: "Thou shalt not steal." They said to Him: The very blessing that had been pronounced upon our father was: "And he shall be as a wild ass of a man: his hand shall be upon everything." . . . But when He came to the Israelites and "at His right hand was a fiery law unto them," they all opened their mouths and said: "All that the Lord hath spoken will we do and obey (*na'aseh v'nishma*)."

In this rabbinic embellishment of Exodus 24:7, the rabbis expand on the strange phrasing of what the children of Israel said at the foot of Mount Sinai. As the entire nation enters into and accepts the divine covenant, the people promise God *na'aseh v'nishma*, which literally translated means "we will do and we will hear." The priority of *doing* the commandments over *hearing* the commandments deeply puzzled the rabbis and required explanation. Logically, of course, one must hear the commandments before one can do them. In the above-quoted midrash, the seemingly strange and impossible promise of the children of Israel is imaginatively compared to other hypothetical answers to God's invitation. The common feature in each of the other responses is the insistence on viewing the decision to accept the covenant as an opportunity to promote self-interest. Each of the other nations is told the specific content of a commandment and responds to God that it is inconsistent with its own preconceived preferences and identity. The children of Israel, by contrast, at the crucial moment of the founding of the nation, recognize that their identity from that point on is defined by acceptance of the divine commandments. To the rabbinic imagination, it would have made no sense whatsoever for the Israelites to have heard and evaluated the specific content of the divine revelation before accepting. The general promise of the existence of the 613 commandments was sufficient. In this midrash, the rabbis recognized that the search for meaning as exemplified in faith (*na'aseh*) must come before its actual discovery (*nishma*). Returning to the language of this chapter, we can restate their observation as follows: From a religious perspective, the logic of appropriateness must subsume the logic of self-interest. We can summarize this discussion by simply noting that economists are correct to point out that it would often pay to purchase a conscience, but what they fail to notice is the obvious fact that consciences are not for sale.

Conclusion

This chapter attempts to explain why we often fail at business ethics. The answer suggested is that perhaps we have not taken the logic of appropriateness seriously enough. In this connection, consider the following powerful thought experiment suggested by a sociologist of knowledge, Peter L. Berger (1970, p. 54):

> A child wakes up in the night, perhaps from a bad dream, and finds himself surrounded by darkness, alone, beset by nameless threats. At such a moment the contours of trusted reality are blurred or invisible, and in the terror of incipient chaos the child cries out for his mother. It is hardly an exaggeration to say that, at this moment, the mother is being invoked as a high priestess of protective order. It is she (and, in many cases, she alone) who has the power to banish the chaos and to restore the benign shape of the world. And, of course, any good mother will do just that.... She will speak or sing to the child, and the content of this communication will invariably be the same—"Don't be afraid—everything is in order, everything is all right." If all goes well, the child will be reassured, his trust in reality recovered, in this trust he will return to sleep.

All of this, of course, belongs to the most routine experiences of life and does not depend upon any religious pre-
conceptions. Yet this common scene raises a far from ordinary question, which immediately introduces a religious
dimension: *Is the mother lying to the child?* [emphasis added]

I believe that Akerlof's view described above, and all views
grounded ultimately on individual self-interest, entail a positive
answer to this question. Berger is surely correct when he concludes (pp. 54–55):

> The answer, in the most profound sense, can be "no" only
> if there is some truth in the religious interpretation of human
> existence. Conversely, if the "natural" is the only reality
> there is, the mother is lying to the child—lying out of love,
> to be sure, and obviously not lying to the extent that her
> reassurance is grounded in the fact of this love—but, in the
> final analysis, lying all the same. Why? Because the reassur-
> ance, transcending the immediately present two individuals
> and their situation, implies a statement of reality as such.

The remainder of this work begins with the assumption that
the mother is not lying. The "natural" is not the only reality there
is. It is with this statement of faith in mind that we begin to
explore the foundations of a Jewish business ethics.

PART II

FOUNDATIONS

So God created man in His own image, in the image of God created He him, male and female created He them. And God blessed them and God said unto them, be fruitful and multiply, and fill the earth and subdue it, and have dominion over the fish of the sea, over the fowl of the heaven, and over the beasts, and all over the earth.

(Genesis 1:27–28)

And the eternal God formed the man of the dust of the ground and breathed into his nostrils the breath of life, and man became a living soul. And the eternal God planted a garden eastward in Eden. . . . And the eternal God took the man and placed him in the Garden of Eden to serve it and to keep it.   (Genesis 2:7–15)

3

The Goals of A Jewish Business Ethics

The Talmud suggests that the first question asked in the world-to-come is, "Have you been honorable in business?" (Shabbat 31a). To anyone familiar with this source or any of the hundreds of similar Jewish sources relating to business, it is self-evident that the Jewish tradition has historically emphasized the centrality of a business ethics. Judaism has consistently demanded honesty and integrity in all business dealings. Jewish teachings, from the very earliest, have constantly urged us to meet the needs of the least-well-off members of society, "for you yourselves were strangers in the land of Egypt" (Leviticus 19:34).

Nevertheless, it is not obvious what a fully articulated Jewish business ethics might entail. As business transactions continue to become more complex, unique questions emerge. For example, is Judaism opposed to insider trading? If so, on what basis? What are the legitimate goals of a business corporation? Is the capitalist system consistent with Jewish values? The study of Jewish business ethics does not represent a search for final and definitive answers to these questions. No book or code exists where one can look up the answers. As my students often remind me, there are no right and wrong answers. But it is the assumption of this book that a creative and grounded interpretation of Jewish sources can help us to formulate better, more appropriate, and more nuanced responses to these and similar questions.

The interpretive task is a communal responsibility. Interpretation is a discussion we have with each other. This book is my response to, and interpretation of, the many historical and contemporary writers and thinkers who have grappled with Jewish business ethics texts. It will have been successful only if it elicits formal or informal responses from readers.

The purpose of this chapter is to explicitly articulate three goals of a Jewish business ethics. The emphasis here is on introducing some of the important biblical, talmudic, and post-talmudic texts that deal with business ethics. As the discussion will show, Judaism's traditional texts discuss an amazing variety of issues emphasizing responsibilities in the business context. These texts are both legalistic and aspirational. An important theme of this chapter is that an authentic Jewish business ethics will grow out of an understanding of the needs of modern, complex economies but need not accept the status quo as binding. Jewish business ethics texts provide rules of behavior, but more importantly, they reveal a vision encouraging us to incorporate the highest human and spiritual ideals into the ordinary world of business.

The Goals of Jewish Business Ethics

Ideally, Jewish business ethics should—

1. help us develop guidelines for individual behavior and inform our goals and aspirations as business men and women;

2. help us understand appropriate behavior for business organizations; and

3. provide a foundation to critique the justice of national and international economic systems.

These goals are designed to focus attention on three levels of analysis. Separating the goals of business ethics in this way is important because responsibilities at one level may not fit at other levels. For example, it may not be obvious how to jump from the individual employer's responsibility to treat all employees fairly to the corporation's responsibility to employees. The individual may have one set of responsibilities, and the business corporation may have an altogether different role to play. In this instance, individuals may be expected to have more stringent responsibilities than a profit-making business enterprise.

The Role of The Individual

Jewish business texts have traditionally focused primarily (but certainly not exclusively) on the individual's ethical responsibilities. The biblical vision of man is set out clearly in the first two chapters of Genesis. Rabbi Joseph B. Soloveitchik, in his path-breaking essay *The Lonely Man of Faith* (1965), has emphasized two distinct descriptions of man's creation. In chapter 1 (vv. 27–28) Genesis reads:

> So God Created man in His own image, in the image of God created He him, male and female created He them. And God blessed them, and God said unto them, "Be fruitful and multiply, and fill the earth and subdue it, and have dominion over the fish of the sea, over the fowl of the heaven, and over the beasts, and all over the earth."

By contrast, in the account in Genesis 2 (vv. 7–15) differs substantially.

> And the eternal God formed the man of the dust of the ground and breathed into his nostrils the breath of life, and man became a living soul. And the eternal God planted a garden eastward in Eden. . . . And the eternal God took the man and placed him in the Garden of Eden to serve it and to keep it.

Rabbi Soloveitchik (1965, p. 10) believes that the different biblical descriptions of man capture his dual nature. "The two accounts deal with two Adams, two men, two fathers of mankind, two types, two representatives of humanity, and it is no wonder that they are not identical." According to this reading of Genesis, the key to understanding the first Adam is the biblical mandate to "subdue the earth"; the key to the second Adam derives from his responsibilities to "serve it and to keep it." Soloveitchik (p. 39) further states:

> The community-fashioning gesture of Adam the first is . . . purely utilitarian and intrinsically egotistic and, as such, rules out sacrificial gestures. For Adam the second, communicating and communing are redemptive sacrificial gestures. Thus, in crisis and distress there was planted the seed of a new type of community—the faith community which reached full fruition in the covenant between God and Abraham.

The wisdom of Soloveitchik's interpretation, and the great insight of Judaism, is its ability to recognize the legitimacy of both Adam the first and Adam the second simultaneously. Describing Adam the first, Soloveitchik (p. 32) writes approvingly, "The natural community fashioned by Adam the first is a work community, committed to the successful production, distribution, and consumption of goods, material as well as cultural." Although a very different portrait emerges when he describes Adam the second, Rabbi Soloveitchik (pp. 41–42) also writes approvingly: Adam the second "hears not only the rhythmic sound of the production line, but also the rhythmic beat of hearts starved for existential companionship and all-embracing sympathy." The two views recorded in Genesis do not derive from "an alleged dual tradition but in dual man, not in an imaginary contradiction between two versions, but in a real contradiction in the nature of man" (p. 10).

The goal of Judaism is not to remake man by ignoring his dual character. Judaism, even while recognizing man's dual nature,

provides a mechanism, or better a path, for man to evolve and bring together his seemingly contradictory natures. Rabbi Abraham Joshua Heschel (1965, p. 41) correctly noted that "to insist that I must be only what I am now is a restriction which human nature must abhor. The being of a person is never completed, final. The status of a person is a *status nascendi*. The choice is made moment by moment." Judaism, at its best, promises a synthesis between the first and second Adams. Again, Rabbi Soloveitchik (p. 84) accurately describes the process.

> The *Halakhah* [Jewish law] believes that there is only one world—not divisible into secular and hallowed sectors—which can either plunge into ugliness and hatefulness, or be roused to meaningful, redeeming activity, gathering up all latent powers into a state of holiness. Accordingly, the task of covenantal man is to be engaged not in dialectical surging forward and retreating, but in uniting the two communities into one community where man is both creative free agent, and obedient servant of God.

Given the Bible's understanding of the dual nature of man, it is not surprising that there are two sets of norms in the texts related to business and economics. I describe the first set of norms as "legalistic," and the second as "models of aspiration." The two sets of norms are consistent with Rabbi Soloveitchick's descriptions of Adam the first and Adam the second, respectively. Legalistic norms attempt to harness man's legitimate mandate to "subdue the earth." They correspond to a perception of man as utilitarian and egotistic, and at their best create a social environment conducive to the "successful production, distribution, and consumption of goods."

The legalistic norms embodied in biblical, talmudic, and post-talmudic texts form the bedrock moral foundation of Judaism's business ethics. While recognizing that there are other ways to interpret Jewish sources, it is impossible to ignore their role as the basic building blocks for a viable Jewish society. The legalistic norms are a floor below which one may not fall.

The existence of legalistic norms, in the sense I am discussing here, distinguishes a Jewish business ethics from some major currents in contemporary academic business ethics. For example, Michael C. Jensen and William H. Meckling (1994, p. 7), pioneers in modern finance and agency theory, unabashedly describe human beings as follows:

> Like it or not, individuals are willing to sacrifice a little of almost anything we care to name, even reputation or morality, for a sufficiently large quantity of other desired things, and these things do not have to be money or even material goods. Moreover, the fact that all individuals make trade-offs (or substitute in virtually every dimension imaginable) means that there are no such things as human "needs" in the sense that word is often used. *There are only human wants, desires, or, in the economist's language, demands* [emphasis added].

Although Jensen and Meckling continue to invoke the language of morality, the context in which they use it unquestionably changes its traditional meaning. For Jensen and Meckling desire trumps ethics every time. Thus it becomes impossible to evaluate business activities from an ethical perspective. R. Edward Freeman, the father of stakeholder theory, reaches a similar conclusion in this instance despite the wide philosophical and ideological chasm that separates him from Jensen and Meckling. Freeman (1994, p. 418) suggests that it is "time to give up the role of finding some moral bedrock for business."

> Finding such bedrock . . . is especially fruitless on pragmatist grounds *for there are no foundations for either business or ethics* [emphasis added]. All we have is our own history, culture, institutions, and our imaginations. For the pragmatist it is "just us" rather than "justice" or "justification" in any sense of foundational bedrock. The cash value of our metaphors and narratives just is how they enable us to live, and the proof is in the living.

A business ethics grounded in traditional Jewish teachings cannot assent to either of the above-quoted views.

While necessary, legalistic norms alone are not sufficient. Models of aspiration, the second set of norms, are compatible with the biblical responsibility to "serve it and keep it." The implicit assumption underlying these norms is that man is "starved for existential companionship and all-embracing sympathy." Models of aspiration demand, not simply obedience to a set of fixed texts, but an imaginative and all-encompassing attempt to transform ourselves. Models of aspiration point to the heavens above.

The distinction between these two sets of norms has been described by Walter Wurzburger (1994, p. 3):

> From my perspective, *Halakhah* represents not merely "the way of God"—that is, a divinely revealed body of laws; it also functions as a way to God, leading not necessarily to mystical union with Him, but to a life dedicated to responding to Him through obedience to His commandments and imitation of His ways.

Adopting Wurzburger's imagery, legalistic norms are the way "of" God, whereas models of aspiration are the way "to" God. The way to God is anchored in the open-ended biblical commandment to imitate His ways.

To further clarify the difference between legalistic texts and models of aspiration, it is useful to provide some examples of each. Leviticus 19:9–14 provides a concrete example of a legalistic text.

> And when ye reap the harvest of your land, thou shalt not wholly reap the corner of thy field, neither shalt thou gather the gleaning of thy harvest. And thou shalt not glean the vineyard, neither shalt thou gather the fallen fruit of the vineyard, thou shalt leave them for the poor and for the stranger: I am the Lord your God. Ye shall not steal: neither shall ye deal falsely, nor lie one to another. And ye shall not

swear by My name falsely, so that thou profane the name of
thy God: I am the Lord. Thou shalt not oppress thy neighbor, nor rob him; the wages of a hired servant shall not abide
with thee all night until the morning. Thou shall not curse
the deaf, nor put a stumbling block before the blind, but
thou shalt fear thy God: I am the Lord.

The biblical text prohibits farmers from gathering all the
produce of the field. Individuals are prohibited from stealing,
robbing, lying, and "oppressing" one another. Employers are
prohibited from withholding employees' wages overnight. In
addition the text explicitly prohibits the cursing of the deaf and
putting "a stumbling block before the blind." The text twice
invokes the refrain "I am the Lord" and concludes with a warning
"thou shalt fear thy God."

Legalistic norms differ substantially from models of aspiration. As these verses illustrate, legalistic norms are predominantly
(but not exclusively) couched as prohibitions—"thou shalt not . .
." Legalistic norms are generally unambiguous and specific. In
this sense, legalistic norms are like contracts; clearer and more
focused language enhances their usefulness. The explicit motivation for accepting them is fear of God rather than love of God or
imitation of His ways.

Deuteronomy 25:13–16 provides a second example of a legalistic business-related text.

> Thou shalt not have in thy house diverse measures, a
> great and a small. A perfect and just weight shalt thou have;
> a perfect and just measure shalt thou have; that thy days
> may be long upon the land which the Lord thy God giveth
> thee. For all that do such things, even all that do
> unrighteously, are an abomination unto the Lord thy God.

As above, the norm is formulated as a prohibition, although
it is repeated in positive terms. Similar to the Leviticus text, the
language is precise and unambiguous. The reasons provided to

induce obedience, however, are more complex than in the first text. Here, a specific motivation for adopting the rules is provided. First, there is a purely "utilitarian" reason: "that thy days may be long." Second, the text suggests that there is an assumed mutual understanding that the practices prohibited are "an abomination." Despite these differences, it is clear that the motivation is not love of God.

The code of law anticipates particular classes of cases and develops directives to be followed. Other biblical examples of legalistic norms include Exodus 20:13, Exodus 22:24, and Exodus 23:4. These and other verses set up general rules which are then applied on a case-by-case basis. Individual cases share enough similar characteristics to make this approach viable. Aharon Lichtenstein (1978), in an important article titled "Does Jewish Tradition Recognize an Ethic Independent of *Halakha*?", further amplifies that legalistic judgments are essentially grounded in deductive reasoning. "Metaphors that speak of laws as controlling or governing a case," he says (1978, p. 115), "are therefore perfectly accurate." He clarifies (ibid.):

> The formalist is guided by a principle or a rule governing a category of cases defined by a number of characteristics. The more sensitive and sophisticated the system, the more individuated the categories. Whatever the degree of specificity, however, the modus operandi is the same: action grows out of the application of class rules to a particular case judged to be an instance of that class or of the interaction of several classes, there being, of course principles to govern seemingly hybrid cases as well.

Selected Biblical Sources: Models of Aspiration

The texts discussed in the preceding section differ in important ways from the four examples of models of aspiration that follow. The selection is designed to be illustrative rather than exhaustive.

> Thou shalt not covet thy neighbor's house; thou shalt not covet thy neighbor's wife, nor his man-servant, nor his maid-servant, nor his ox, nor his ass, nor any thing that is thy neighbor's.
>
> (Exodus 20:14)
>
> Thou shalt not take vengeance nor bear any grudge against the children of My people, but thou shalt love thy neighbor as thyself: I am the Lord.
>
> (Leviticus 19:18)
>
> The stranger that sojourneth with you shall be unto you as the home-born among you, and thou shalt love him as thyself; for ye were strangers in the land of Egypt.
>
> (Leviticus 19:34)
>
> The Lord will establish thee for a holy people unto Himself, as He hath sworn unto thee; if thou shalt keep the commandments of the Lord thy God, and walk in His ways.
>
> (Deuteronomy 28:9)

Rather than place us in our final destination, these texts point us in a direction—"and walk in His ways." They demand not only actions, but states of mind. The texts prohibit jealousy and hatred, but above all, the essential characteristic is love of our fellow man, even the stranger.

The Bible's models of aspiration are generally (but not always) formulated in the positive: "thou shalt love him as thyself." The texts are open-ended and more ambiguous than legal norms. It is by no means obvious what "love thy neighbor" will mean in any given case (although it probably is much easier to know what it does not mean). The motivation here, as in Leviticus 19:18, is often the ability to sympathize with the stranger based on historical memory, "for ye were strangers in the land of Egypt." If the legalistic norms are correctly thought of as contractual obligations, the texts cited here are covenantal. The hallmark of such a relationship is the personal and communal transformation that it entails. The covenant itself makes us. When one enters into a covenant, one enters into community. Wurzburger (1994, p. 15) clarifies this distinction:

I look upon *Halakhah* as an indispensable component but not as coextensive with the full range and scope of the Jewish normative system. I deliberately avoid the term "*Halakhic* Ethics," preferring to speak of "Covenant Ethics." In my view, Jewish ethics encompasses not only outright *halakhic* rules governing the area of morality, but also intuitive moral responses arising from the Covenantal relationship with God, which provides the matrix for forming ethical ideals not necessarily patterned after legal models. To use Erich Fromm's terminology, Judaism provides for an "ethics of responsibility" as well as for an "ethics of duty" or an "ethics of obedience."

The approach of Martin Buber, especially in *I and Thou*, is revealing in this context. Although Buber's staunch rejection of legal norms is not consistent with the view discussed to this point, there is much to be learned about models of aspiration from his powerful advocacy of the I-Thou relationship. Buber (1958, pp. 31–33) writes:

To man the world is twofold, in accordance with his twofold attitude.

He perceives what exists round about him—simply things, and beings as things; and what happens round about him— simply events, and actions as events; things consisting of qualities, events of moments; things entered in the graph of place, events in that of time, things and events bounded by other things and events, measured by them, comparable with them: he perceives an ordered and detached world. . . Its organisation can be surveyed and brought out again and again; gone over with closed eyes, and verified with open eyes. . . .

Or on the other hand, man meets what exists and becomes as what is over against him, always simply a *single* being and each thing simply as being. What exists is opened to him in happenings, and what happens affects him as what is. Nothing is present for him except this one being, but it implicates the whole world. Measure and comparison have disappeared; it lies with yourself how much of the immeasurable becomes reality for you. These meetings are not organised to make the world, but each is a sign of the world-order. . . . Between you and it there is mutual giving: you say *Thou* to it and give yourself to it, it says *Thou* to you and gives itself to you.

The great myth of business ethics is that business men and women, acting in their roles of business men and women, possess legalistic norms exclusively. We often behave as if we were unaware of Hillel's famous summary dictum, "What is hateful to you, do not to your neighbor" (Shabbat 31a). In the "real" world, so the argument goes, the models of aspiration do not apply. Obedience to specific legal norms is sufficient. Love is "nice," but irrelevant to the bottom line. As the myth would have it, we live in two unbridgeable worlds. Our working lives are dominated by an exclusively utilitarian and legalistic ethic. In our "free" time, we have the leisure to pursue personal and individualistic goals. In our free time, if we so choose, we enjoy covenantal living.

A student of mine, as part of a business ethics assignment, recently described this worldview as follows:

There is a real business world out there and people have to outmaneuver each other. If one is more successful than the other, it does not mean that the person was being unethical. It just implies that the person was more witty than his competitors. People are interested in making more money than the next guy; nobody is interested in being more ethical than the next guy.

Whatever the merits of this view might be as a description of the way we actually live, it falls well short of Jewish ideals. In other words, while the myth may have some descriptive validity (although the extent of its validity is debatable), it has no normative power. Numerous talmudic texts support this claim. Leo Jung (1978, p. 135) demonstrates the point as follows:

The Talmud has a very telling illustration of the high standards taken for granted, especially by scholars. Rabbi Safra, a Babylonian scholar and merchant, famous for exceeding scrupulousness, is cited as an example of one "who speaketh truth in his heart," who says what he truly means. He was once praying whilst a buyer offered him a price for some goods. Unwilling to interrupt his devotions, he would not answer. The buyer, mistaking his silence for unwillingness to accept the offer, increased the price. As Rabbi Safra concluded the prayer, he accepted the first offer, saying that he would have assented and that his silence was misunderstood.

Another good example of the necessity to synthesize and temper legal norms with models of aspiration is a case cited in the talmudic tractate of Sotah (21b). This rabbinic text embellishes and clarifies the prohibition in Leviticus 19 of "reaping the corner of the field" quoted above. (See also Leviticus 23:22 and Deuteronomy 24:19.) The talmudic rabbis taught:

> What is the "cunning rogue" like? . . . He who gives a poor man a dinar to bring his possessions to the total of two hundred zuz, for we have learnt; he who possesses two hundred zuz may not take gleanings, forgotten sheaves, the produce of the corner of the field, or the poor tithe; but should he lack one dinar of the two hundred [zuz], even if a thousand persons give him [the gleanings, etc.] simultaneously, he may accept.

Leviticus 19 requires interpretation. Who are these "poor" who can legally and correctly demand the "corner of the field"? The Bible does not offer a complete definition of what constitutes poverty, nor should one expect it. Poverty is necessarily a function of contemporary social conditions. Nevertheless, the rabbis of the talmudic period, in their attempt to apply the law, required specificity. Any individual whose wealth fell below the 200-zuz level was "poor," and therefore eligible for communal assistance. If the person's wealth was exactly 200 zuz or above, he was disqualified from receiving help. This is precisely the way a well-functioning legal system must, of necessity, operate.

Society recognizes the need to articulate clear and unambiguous rules. In this instance, the 200-zuz cutoff necessarily introduces an element of arbitrariness into the system. If a man who is one dinar short of 200 zuz is poor, does any judge really believe that the same man with the additional dinar is materially better off? The overarching demand for specific rules opens up the possibility for abusing the legal system. The existence of cunning rogues, who spend a dinar to remove their legal responsibility, is not a failure of this specific law, or of the legal system in general, but cunning rogues are a necessary "cost" of all purely legal codes. The cunning rogue may indeed remove a legal barrier, but unquestionably still possesses ethical responsibilities. The talmudic case teaches the idea that workable legal rulings must be embedded in a culture which recognizes models of aspiration. This case provides a clear example of the talmudic process of synthesizing law and ethics (see Friedman 1985 for additional examples).

The Role of the Organization

The texts examined thus far speak about the responsibilities of the individual. While discussion of individual responsibilities remains an important topic to business ethicists, moral issues related to the profit-making business enterprise are becoming more urgent. Managers, board members, employees, and investors are increasingly confronted by business decisions with social and therefore ethical implications.

As our economy begins to spill over domestic borders, as corporations continue to expand in size, as technological impacts multiply, society's well-being becomes more tightly linked with corporate decision making. Simply put, as corporate power increases, the ramifications of the actions of corporations multiply. Many of the most important ethical decisions individuals face occur in the corporate context. The executive decisions that ultimately led to the *Exxon Valdez* disaster were surely not only economic decisions (even if that is how they were framed by the principal actors), but also involved an ethical component. The question of whether or not a beer distillery should specifically target urban areas for a high-alcohol malt liquor must be answered both with economic and ethical criteria. The decision whether to continue marketing or to withdraw a record album advocating the killing of police officers, regardless of its solution, does not simply demand recourse to profit considerations, but also requires a formulation, and at least an implicit understanding, of corporate obligations to society (Pava and Krausz, 1995).

The twentieth century has seen an unprecedented growth in the size, importance, and power of corporations. Large corporations have proven to be extremely efficient at producing goods and services. It is the success of the corporation that has necessitated the development of the idea of corporate social responsibility.

Adolf A. Berle Jr. and Gardiner C. Means, both at Columbia University, were among the earliest business researchers to explain and formally document the revolutionary changes taking place in the U.S. economy. In *The Modern Corporation and Private Property*, a highly influential book published in 1933, they warned readers about the increasing power of corporate managers (p. 353).

> Such a great concentration of power and such a diversity of interest raise the long-fought issue of power and its regulation—of interest and its protection. A constant warfare has existed between the individuals wielding power, in whatever form, and the subjects of that power. Just as there is a continuous desire for power, so also there is a continuous desire to make that power the servant of the bulk of the individuals it affects. . . . Absolute power is useful in building the organization. More slow, but equally sure is the development of social pressure demanding that the power

shall be used for the benefit of all concerned. This pressure, constant in ecclesiastical and political history, is already making its appearance in many guises in the economic field.

Further, Berle and Means carefully noted the failure of traditional views of the corporation (p. 354).

> By tradition, a corporation "belongs" to its shareholders . . . and theirs is the only interest to be recognized as the object of corporate activity. Following this tradition, and without regard for the changed character of ownership, it would be possible to apply in the interests of the passive property owner the doctrine of strict property rights. . . . By application of this doctrine, the group in control of a corporation would be placed in a position of trusteeship in which it would be called on to operate or arrange for the operation of the corporation for the sole benefit of the security owners despite the fact that the latter have ceased to have power over or to accept responsibility for the active property in which they have an interest. Were this course followed, the bulk of American industry might soon be operated by trustees for the sole benefit of inactive and irresponsible security owners.

Berle and Means concluded their study with prophetic accuracy. They wrote (p. 356), "Neither the claims of ownership nor those of control can stand against the paramount interests of the community."

In a later work, Berle (1954, p. 114) clarified more boldly. In order to meet the demands of society, corporations need to demonstrate self-restraint. Although Berle chose to use the term "corporate conscience," his view unquestionably represents an important early articulation of corporate social responsibility.

> So, it seems, the corporations have a conscience, or else accept direction from the conscience of the government.

This conscience must be built into institutions so that it can be invoked as a right by the individuals and interests subject to the corporate power. It may not be christened with a Latin name; its keeper may not be called "Chancellor," the place where the conscience can be called into action will no longer be called the Curia Regis. But, as at Runnymede through Magna Carta, it will be required to be present and reachable. It will be required to observe certain rules designed for the protection of individuals.

Berle's view is correct. In fact, much of the history of corporate social responsibility has been an attempt to experiment with alternative ways of institutionalizing the corporate conscience. Individuals and groups, both inside and outside the corporation, have recognized the special status of corporations and their unique social responsibilities. These business leaders and critics have tried to formulate a coherent view of the corporation which attempts to take both the profit motive and legitimate social goals seriously.

In spite of the importance of introducing the notion of social responsibility into the corporation, it is by no means a trivial task. Richard T. De George, a leading researcher on contemporary business ethics, has noted the discontinuity of moving from individual ethics to organizational ethics (see also Goodpaster and Mathews 1982, French 1977). He writes (1986, p. 423):

Business ethics is more than the application of general ethical theories to cases or issues in business. Those involved in business ethics both apply general ethical theories and test ways to expand the theories. They also raise difficulties that force a rethinking of portions of the general theories. For instance, one of the important issues to have emerged is whether, to what extent, and in what way corporations can or should be held morally responsible. Are they simply organizations and artifacts that should be controlled, are they moral entities or quasi-moral entities with rights, or do they have some other status and are they to be viewed in some other light? The answers to these questions are not supplied by general ethical theory, which traditionally has been concerned with the actions of human individuals. The meaning of responsibility, clearly, must be changed if it can be appropriately applied to corporations (or nations, etc.) as well as to human persons.

Underscoring the difficulty of defining the precise contours of corporate responsibilities is a recent *Business Week* cover story (Aug. 1, 1994) featuring Levi Strauss and Co.'s unique managerial philosophy. Levis Strauss, a privately held corporation, is the world's largest apparel maker. The title of the article asks the question, "Is Levis Strauss' Approach Visionary—or Flaky?" What makes Levi Strauss's philosophy unique, and apparently what prompted *Business Week*'s query, is the belief of the firm's chief executive officer that "the corporation should be an ethical creature—an organism capable of both reaping profits and making the world a better place to live." Levi Strauss's vision is summarized through its corporate credo, authored by top management:

NEW BEHAVIORS
Management must exemplify "directness, openness to influence, commitment to the success of others, and willingness to acknowledge our own contributions to problems."
DIVERSITY
Levi's "values a diverse workforce (age, sex, ethnic group, etc.) at all levels of the organization. . . . Differing points of view will be sought; diversity will be valued and honestly rewarded, not suppressed."
RECOGNITION
Levi's will "provide greater recognition—both financial and psychic—for individuals and teams that contribute to our success. . . those who create and innovate and those who continually support day-to-day business requirements."

ETHICAL MANAGEMENT PRACTICES

Management should epitomize "the stated standards of ethical behavior. We must provide clarity about our expectations and must enforce these standards throughout the corporation."

COMMUNICATIONS

Management must be "clear about company, unit, and individual goals and performance. People must know what is expected of them and receive timely, honest feedback . . ."

EMPOWERMENT

Management must "increase the authority and responsibility of those closest to our products and customers. By actively pushing the responsibility, trust, and recognition into the organization, we can harness and release the capabilities of all our people."

The values inherent in the credo are not merely a public relations tool. They are reflected in specific corporate actions as follows:

1. Levi's board voted unanimously to pull $40 million of business out of China in protest of human-rights violations.

2. All Levi's employees are subject to a 360-degree review process. Employees are evaluated by superiors, peers, and subordinates.

3. In remaking its product development and distribution systems, Levi's asked 6,000 employees for input. The company's diversity council, representing minority interests, was included in the process.

4. Levi's has significantly increased the number of minority and women managers. More than half of its managers are women.

5. The company's plants are rated some of the safest in the industry.

6. The company does not employ children below the age of fourteen in its overseas operations.

Many of these actions can and have been defended along traditional strategic lines and therefore are not controversial. Improving employee evaluation procedures is simply sound business. Increasing the diversity of the workforce and enhancing communication between managers and employees will undoubtedly lead to improved long-run financial performance. Justifying corporate social responsibility activities through traditional economic criteria is important. The suggestion that corporate social responsibility can lead to increased shareholder value in no way diminishes the social benefits accruing from these activities and provides a strong and noncontroversial basis to legitimate them. Nevertheless, improved financial performance is neither a necessary nor a sufficient condition to justify social responsibility activities. Levi's costly decision to pull out of China in response to human rights violations may indeed prove to be the correct decision from a strategic perspective. It would seem, however, that this decision should not have been, and was not, motivated solely by profit considerations. Understanding Levi's decision necessarily requires us to adopt the language of ethics and responsibility. Does Levi Strauss & Co. have an ethical responsibility to refrain from doing business with human rights violators? Levi's managers believe the answer is yes.

Jewish writings have traditionally been cognizant of the distinction between private and public responsibilities. For example, Aaron Levine (1993), basing himself on the work of Rabbi Hayyim Soloveitchik (1853–1918), suggests that Judaism's charity obligation consists of both a public and a private component. He argues that the repetition of the biblical commandment to "uphold the poor" (Leviticus 25:35) and to "open thy hand" to the needy (Deuteronomy 15:7–8) reflects the dual nature of the charity obligation. "The Leviticus passage refers to society's collective responsibility to relieve poverty, while the Deuteronomy passage speaks of the individual's personal charity obligation" (p. 202).

Nevertheless, few Jewish sources focus explicitly on the level of organizational responsibilities. The limited number of texts is not unexpected. The existence of large business organizations is a modern phenomenon, and Jewish ethical texts evolved before the ascendancy of the large corporation. Does this fact, however, necessarily imply that a Jewish business ethics must remain silent about organizational ethics? Is one compelled, even if against one's will, to assent to Milton Friedman's view (1962, p. 12) that the "really important ethical problems are those that face an individual in a free society"? Fortunately, the answers to these questions are an emphatic no. A Jewish business ethics can and must recognize that organizational issues provide some of the most important and fertile ground for a discussion of business ethics. If Jewish business ethics is to provide a complete and meaningful structure, it must provide a relevant organizational ethics.

Unquestionably, Aaron Levine's important contributions to Jewish business ethics (1980, 1987, 1993, 1994) have provided the strongest support for this contention. In comparing a pure free-market ideology to Jewish sources, Levine (1994, p. 2) concludes that "Capitalism provides . . . no mechanism which forces market participants to give pause and consider the worthiness of their economic activity on anything other than an economic criterion. In contrast to the capitalist ethic, Torah idealism requires an economic actor to consider the inherent worthiness of his actions." Specifically, Levine (1994, p. 2) argues for the existence of a biblical "charge to man for self-actualization in realizing his God-like potential as a creative being." Levine concludes this discussion by carefully extending Judaism's prohibition of gambling from the level of the individual to that of the organization.

Levine's primary textual supports focus on individual prohibitions. Maimonides (Egypt, 1135–1204) and Rabbi Joseph Caro (Israel, 1488–1575) both held that gambling earnings were a form of theft by dint of a rabbinical expansion of the laws of *gezel* (robbery). Other medieval Jewish authorities prohibited gambling, not as a form of theft, but because it is an inherently wasteful activity. The latter view suggests that gambling activities do not contribute to the settlement of the world (*yishuv ha'olam*). Neither view would explicitly prohibit an organization from engaging in or promoting gambling activities. Levine's contribution is his cautious but powerful interpretation and extension of these texts to the organizational level. In his words (1994, p. 2):

> Gambling is . . . an unredeeming activity. It is either *avak gezel* or an activity which contributes nothing to *yishuv ha'olam*. . . . To be sure, Halakhah may be incapable of making a case . . . to prohibit investing in the stock of a gambling corporation or to prohibit the manufacture and sale of gambling equipment.
>
> But [the mandate to realize God-like potential] would recommend a definite shifting away from these activities.

Similarly, Levine questions the legitimacy of the tobacco industry and the manufacture and sale of war toys.

In addition to Levine, Meir Tamari has made important contributions to Jewish business ethics. In *With All Your Possessions: Jewish Ethics and Economic Life* (1987), Tamari interprets and extends the talmudic discussion of damages to issues related to environmental responsibilities. He writes (p. 279):

> There is a moral and ethical dimension involved in preventing damage to other people's persons or property—or, for that matter, even to one's own person or property. Sometimes the conception of such damage in purely economic terms tends to obscure this aspect of these environmental issues—yet it remains an important part of our values system. . . . Such an outlook on life accepts that there are factors in the world over and above man's right to private property and to the creation of material goods, even in a legitimate manner.

Specifically, Tamari cites the talmudic view that an individual who sets an object in motion (e.g., sparks from an anvil, chips from the felling of wood) that indirectly causes damage, even if the final damage is spread by natural causes, such as wind, is held liable. He argues that this legal ruling can be extended to the organizational level. "In our day this would seem to apply to the pollution of the atmosphere or water through industrial wastes" (p. 283). Similarly, he cites (p. 290) the following talmudic ruling: "It is necessary to remove [from the confines of the village] the permanent threshing floors [because of the chaff], cemeteries, tanneries [because of the stench], and kilns [because of smoke]" (Bava Batra 2:3). Tamari concludes that this source provides evidence for the suggestion that the ecological needs of the community may take precedence over the property rights of firms to pursue profitable activities.

Levine and Tamari are both engaged in a process of wrestling out of authoritative texts meaningful norms relevant to contemporary business organizations. They ask us to alter considerably the inherited view of the business enterprise, with its exclusive focus on profit maximization. Their views are diametrically opposed to the notion that the only responsibility of business is to increase its profits (Friedman 1970).

Jewish business ethics, at the organizational level, constitutes strong evidence against the widely held myth, discussed above, that business norms can be based solely on a legalistic approach. Levine and Tamari both invoke, either explicitly or implicitly, the distinction articulated above between legal texts and models of aspirations. Levine, for example, consistent with our vocabulary, explicitly suggests that while there may be no specific prohibition in halakhah against investing in gambling stocks, the authoritative texts recommend shifting away from gambling activities.

Levine and Tamari provide a good first step, yet much more work at the organizational level is required. In order to develop Jewish business ethics, especially (but not exclusively) at the level of the organization, models of aspiration will of necessity play an integral role. A Jewish business ethics which conceptualizes Judaism as merely a set of legal rules is bound to fail. Jewish business ethics needs to continue to self-consciously promote models of aspirations, as well as to rely on fixed legal norms.

Certainly, however, it is important to ask whether this is the direction we should head in. Numerous arguments against corporate social responsibility have been put forth: it is a form of taxation without representation; it will lead to fascism; managers have no expertise in fighting social ills. Ethics is subjective, and therefore there will always be disagreements as to the precise contours of corporate social responsibility. Specifically, we ask two questions: Is corporate social responsibility prudent? And do we really want to demand that organizations voluntarily incorporate these "soft" responsibilities? Business men and women surely need to know the "rules of the game," as Albert Z. Carr (1990, p. 73) aptly put it. The very strengths of the models of aspiration are their open-ended language and demand for transformation. These norms are not generally associated with the rough-and-tumble world of business. These questions cannot be ignored.

Levi Strauss was cited above as an example of a company attempting to incorporate aspirational language into the business context. Is it merely coincidental that Levi's is a privately held company, and therefore does not have to answer to irate shareholders and financial analysts? Many argue that it may be well and fine for a privately held corporation like Levi Strauss to invoke ethical language, but public corporations need to focus constantly on the single and unswerving goal of profit maximization. Simply put, corporate social responsibility is not a prudent strategy in competitive markets.

This criticism is a powerful one, and is often taken as self-evident. However, those who have empirically examined the statistical relationship between corporate social responsibility and traditional financial performance have reached a very different conclusion. In *Social Responsibility and Financial Performance: The Paradox of Social Cost* (1995), Joshua Krausz and I surveyed twenty-two research studies designed to examine this question. Our remarkable finding is that only a single study documented a negative association. Most studies either showed that social responsibility was positively related to financial performance or there was no association. We concluded that there is virtually no evidence to suggest that social responsibility causes poor financial performance. Rather, on average, social responsibility may actually improve traditional financial performance.

We do not overstate the conclusion. The issue of prudence is by no means a nonissue. No doubt, some social responsibility activities will indeed lead to a decrease in traditional financial performance. In these cases, careful analysis is required to legitimate the activities. However, the call for increased social responsibility is ultimately independent of empirical studies documenting positive associations. Do we really want to demand that organizations voluntarily incorporate "soft" responsibilities? This question is the crucial one. From a Jewish perspective, we answer in the affirmative. Rabbi Abraham Joshua Heschel's point (1955, p. 296) is illuminating and authoritative here:

> The dichotomy of faith and works which presented such an important problem in Christian theology was never a problem in Judaism. To us, the basic problem is neither what is the right action nor what is the right intention. The basic problem is: what is right living? And life is indivisible. The inner sphere is never isolated from outward activities. Deed and thought are bound into one. All a person thinks and feels enters everything he does, and all he does is involved in everything he thinks and feels. . . . Right living is like a work of art, the product of a vision and of a wrestling with concrete situations.

Judaism encompasses all aspects of life. Everything one does is informed by legal texts and models of aspiration. "Life is indivisible," or as we put it above, Judaism, at its best, promises a synthesis. The legitimate goals of the business enterprise ultimately need to correspond to and to reinforce the deepest and most important values of Judaism.

The Role of the Economy

For many readers, the third goal of a Jewish business ethics— to serve as a foundation from which to critique the appropriateness of national and international economic systems—is much more familiar than the interpretation and application of organizational ethics discussed above. Comparing authoritative Jewish texts, imbued with idealistic yearnings, to existing economies reminds us that current realities might be different. Jews daily complete their prayers with the hope that "the world shall be perfected under the reign of the Almighty" (*Alenu* hymn). While this and similar texts do not always show us how to get from here to there, they serve an important function. A focus on Jewish texts provides needed critical distance from current economic and political realities. Abraham's plea to God, "Shall not the Judge of all the earth do justly?" (Genesis 18:26), has, more often than not, been redirected, in the Jewish sources, to focus on man's requirement to do justly. The biblical commandment, "Justice, justice shalt thou follow, that thou mayest live, and inherit the land which the Lord thy God giveth thee" (Deuteronomy 16:20), is a permanent call to improve society.

A Jewish business ethics which fully endorses any existing version of capitalism or socialism would fall well short of traditional Jewish ideals. The innovative idea of a jubilee year, with the inspiring mandate to "proclaim liberty throughout the land" (Leviticus 25:10), for example, cannot easily fit into capitalistic or socialistic ideologies.

> And ye shall hallow the fiftieth year, and proclaim liberty throughout the land unto all the inhabitants thereof; it shall be a jubilee unto you; and ye shall return every man unto his possession, and ye shall return every man unto his family. A jubilee shall that fiftieth year be unto you; ye shall not sow, neither reap that which groweth of itself in it, nor gather the grapes in it of the undressed vines. For it is a jubilee; it shall be holy unto you; ye shall eat the increase thereof out of the field. In this year of jubilee ye shall return every man unto his possession. And if thou sell aught unto thy neighbour, or buy of thy neighbor's hand, ye shall not wrong one another. According to the number of years after the jubilee thou shalt

buy of thy neighbor, and according unto the number of years of the crops he shall sell unto thee. According to the multitude of the years thou shalt increase the price thereof, and according to the fewness of the years thou shall diminish the price of it: for the number of crops doth he sell unto thee. And ye shall not wrong one another; but thou shalt fear thy God; for I am the Lord your God. Wherefore ye shall do My statutes, and keep Mine ordinances and do them; and ye shall dwell in safety.

It is not insignificant that some of the most sublime prophetic messages focus on issues related to business and economics. The rabbis selected the following text from Isaiah (58:5–7) to be read annually on Yom Kippur, the holiest day of the Jewish year:

Can such be My chosen fast, the day of man's self-denial?
To bow down his head like a bulrush, to sit in sackcloth and ashes? Is that what you call fasting, a day acceptable to the Lord?
Behold, this is the fast that I esteem precious:
Loosen the chains of wickedness, undo the bonds of oppression,
Let the crushed go free, break all yokes of tyranny!
Share your food with the hungry, take the poor to your home,
Clothe the naked when you see them, never turn from your fellow.

Similarly, the words of the prophet Amos (8:4–6) continue to echo through the generations.

Hear this, O ye that would swallow the needy
And destroy the poor of the land,
Saying, When will the new moon be gone, that we may sell grain?
And the Sabbath, that we may set forth corn,

Making the ephah small and the shekel great, and falsi-
fying the balances of deceit?
That we may buy the poor for silver,
And the needy for a pair of shoes,
And sell the refuse of the corn.

An authentic Jewish business ethics cannot ignore these texts.
To the contrary, these legal and aspirational norms must be the
starting point of a business ethics appropriate for evaluating
society's economic arrangements. Clearly, any business ethics
that disregards the needs of the least-well-off members of the
community cannot speak in the name of Judaism.

The texts cited thus far allow us to paint a preliminary picture:

* Existing economies can be improved.
* It is meaningful, and not naive, to hope that individuals
are capable of not wronging one another.
* Ritual observances alone are not sufficient.
* Man's ethical activities can potentially make a differ-
ence in the scheme of things.
* Society has responsibilities to the hungry, the poor, and
the needy.

There is an intriguing biblical narrative, often overlooked,
which nicely illustrates how an economic system ought to incorporate justified moral demands asserted even by the disenfran-
chised. During the Israelites' forty-year sojourn in the wilderness,
the five daughters of Zelophehad—Mahlah, Noah, Hoglah, Milcah,
and Tirzah—from the tribe of Manasseh, approached Moses with
the following request to alter the existing laws of inheritance
(Numbers 27:3–7):

"Our father died in the wilderness, and he was not among
the company of them that gathered themselves together
against Korah, but he died in his own sin; and he had no
sons. Why should the name of our father be done away from

among his family, because he had no son? Give unto us a possession among the brethren of our father." And Moses brought their cause before the Lord. And the Lord spoke unto Moses, saying: "The daughters of Zelophehad speak right: thou shalt surely give them a possession of an inheritance among their father's brethren; and thou shalt cause the inheritance of their father to pass unto them."

What makes this episode so unusual is its very inclusion in the biblical text. The Bible chooses to report not only the legal rule but also the circumstances surrounding its promulgation. To understand this narrative is to understand that what counts in the biblical vision is not only the final status of the law, but also the process by which the rulings are reached. In this case, the scope of the law is enlarged only as a result of the daughters' justifiable complaint, "Why should the name of our father be done away from among his family?" A later rabbinic embellishment derives an important and contemporary message. "God's love is not like the love of a mortal father; the latter prefers his sons to his daughters, but He that created the world extends His love to all His children. His tender mercies are over all His works" (as quoted by Hertz 1960, p. 691).

A Jewish business ethics cannot endorse a purely laissez-faire form of capitalism. Nevertheless, it is just as inaccurate to equate Judaism with modern liberalism. Aaron Levine's treatment of minimum wage legislation provides a case in point (1993). The goal of a minimum wage law—to provide a living wage to employees—is completely consistent with Jewish values promoting a communal charity obligation. Further, there is ample precedent in talmudic case law for price controls as a means of promoting societal goals (Bava Batra 90a). However, Levine correctly concludes that economic analysis demonstrates that a minimum wage will not achieve its laudatory goal. In fact, economic analysis suggests that minimum wage legislation might harm those it is designed to help by increasing unemployment among the disadvantaged. Judaism's ideals are aspirational but certainly not quixotic. There is a utopian strand running through Judaism; utopia is something to be dreamed about, prayed for, and worked at. But, in the final analysis, utopia is not yet here.

Conclusion

We conclude this chapter by observing that Judaism recognizes the legitimacy of business, properly conceived. Individuals have a responsibility to conduct themselves in an honest and forthright way. Organizations, even while increasing profits, need to recognize some form of corporate social responsibility. Economic systems need to be perceived as "level playing fields." Most important, however, the constant theme of this chapter has been that business ultimately cannot justify itself. Business is not conducted on some mythical ethically-neutral island. The pursuit of economic well-being, whether at the individual, organizational, or national level, is inextricably enmeshed in a web of ethical values. Neither Adam the first nor Adam the second, as Rabbi Soloveitchik taught, is completely self-sufficient. In this spirit, the Talmud (Avodah Zarah 2b) offers the following trenchant criticism of the Roman Empire:

> In times to come, the Holy One, blessed be He, will take a scroll of the Law in His embrace and proclaim: "Let him who has occupied himself herewith, come and take his reward." . . . the Kingdom of Edom [Rome] will enter first before Him. . . . the Holy One, blessed be He, will then say to them: "Wherewith have you occupied yourselves?" They will reply: . . . "we have established many marketplaces, we have erected many baths, we have accumulated much gold and silver, and all this we did only for the sake of . . . Torah." The Holy One, blessed be He, will say in reply: "You foolish ones among the peoples, all that you have done, you have only done to satisfy your own desires. You have established marketplaces to place courtesans therein, baths to revel in them, [as to the accumulation of] silver and gold that is

Mine, as it is written: `Mine is the silver and Mine is the gold, saith the Lord of Hosts' (Haggai 2:8)."

As this hypothetical conversation illustrates, the satisfaction of desires alone is not a sufficient justification for engaging in economic activities. The author of this rabbinic parable understood the importance of and necessity for marketplaces, baths, gold, and silver. He does not suggest that engaging in secular activities is inappropriate. Rather, the point of a religiously based business ethics is that economic activities are never to be viewed only as ends in themselves. Economic activities—at the individual, organizational, and national level—are a means toward building a just and caring society in which the best of human and spiritual values may flourish.

Commenting on the verse "And the Lord God commanded the man" (Genesis 2;16), Rabbi Soloveitchik (1967, p. 59) noted,

> With the birth of the norm, man becomes aware of his singularly human existence which expresses itself in the dichotomous experience of being unfree, restricted, imperfect and unredeemed, and, at the same time, being potentially powerful, great and exalted, uniquely endowed, capable of rising far above his environment in response to the divine moral challenge.

Too often, in moments of religious fervor, we readily acknowledge the hope of rising above the environment through God's norms only to accept, moments later, the myth that business is value-free. A dialogue centered on interpreting and applying Jewish business texts can serve to remind us that the world we pray in is the very same world in which we do business.

4

The Substance of Jewish Business Ethics

What does a specifically Jewish business ethics entail? Philosophers generally agree that meaningful ethical statements are universal in scope. Immanuel Kant (1724–1804), one of the greatest philosophers of the Western tradition, believed that moral actions must conform to universal principles. Kant (1938, p. 17) formalized this observation through his justly famous categorical imperative, "I am never to act otherwise than so that I could at the same time will that my maxim should become a universal law." If Kant and other philosophers are correct, what sense is there in speaking about a business ethics particular to Judaism? Just as a Jewish algebra or a Jewish physics is a contradiction in terms, so too is the notion of a particularly Jewish business ethics.

The goal of this and the next chapter is to deny the preceding assertion and to explore the potentially unique characteristics of a Jewish business ethics. In the final analysis, ethics is not like algebra or physics. Understanding and acting on our ethical responsibilities as Jews is an altogether different task than creating intellectual and philosophical theories and models. While philosophy and religion have common features, and while each approach can learn and benefit from one another, Jewish ethics differs from purely philosophical approaches in two respects. In terms of both substance and method, Jewish business ethics is unique. The remainder of this chapter focuses on the substance of Jewish business ethics. In chapter 3, the methodology of Jewish ethics is explored.

Jewish Ethics Defined

Specifically, it is argued here that, in terms of substance, Jewish business ethics differs from secular approaches in three very specific ways. Jewish ethics (1) recognizes God as the ultimate source of value, (2) acknowledges the centrality of the community, and (3) holds out the promise that men and women (living in community) can transform themselves.

Like other ethical systems based on theological and religious assumptions, Jewish ethics is an attempt to answer the question "What is God enabling and requiring us to be and to do?" (Gustafson 1984, p. 1). Building on this theocentric view of ethics, we define the study of Jewish ethics as the interpretation of the written and oral Torah to determine what God commands us to be and to do.

God First

Judaism looks to God as the ultimate source of value in our lives. From a religious perspective, the first question in ethics is always about God's values and never about man's desires. This point is powerfully illustrated in Genesis, chapter 22. This narrative has traditionally been interpreted as a defining text of Judaism.

> And it came to pass after these things, that God did prove Abraham, and said unto him: "Abraham"; and he said: "Here am I." And God said: "Take now thy son, thine only son, whom thou lovest, even Isaac, and get thee into the land of Moriah; and offer him there for a burnt-offering upon one of the mountains which I tell thee of."

The Bible records no verbal response by Abraham. Rather the text continues "And Abraham rose early in the morning . . ." (22:3). Abraham accepts God's demand. Abraham acquiesces to the "binding of Isaac," the *akedah.*

One wonders why God's test is constructed in such stark, extreme terms. Could not God have chosen another test, a more moderate one, to prove Abraham? Perhaps God might have asked Abraham to commit an act of theft. Surely, for a man of Abraham's integrity and ethical sense, even the slightest moral breach would have created enormous cognitive dissonance. Or, Job-like, He might have commanded Abraham to renounce all of his worldly wealth and prestige as a proof of his willingness to sacrifice his own welfare. The point, of course, is that the power and purpose of the narrative is inextricably linked to the specific command "take now thy son . . . and offer him there for a burnt-offering" (22:2).

Abraham's willingness to slaughter his son Isaac is inconsistent with any maxim that might become universal. If there is any doubt that the categorical imperative is inconsistent with Abraham's willingness to sacrifice Isaac, Kant himself (as quoted in Fackenheim 1973, p. 22) clarifies:

> Abraham should have replied to this putative divine voice: "That I may not kill my good son is absolutely certain. But that you who appear to me are God is not certain and cannot become certain, even though the voice were to sound from the very heavens." . . . [For] that a voice which one seems to hear cannot be divine one can be certain of . . . in case what is commanded is contrary to moral law. However majestic or supernatural it may appear to be, one must regard it as a deception.

Kant does not rule out the possibility that God can communicate with human beings. Kant does rule out the possibility that God can command an action which contradicts our human understanding of morality.

John Stuart Mill suggested an altogether different approach to assess morality. According to Mill, individuals should choose actions that maximize happiness and minimize pain. To the extent that an act satisfies this maxim, it is moral; to the extent that it fails to satisfy it, it is immoral. Mill's theory, known as utilitarianism, continues to exert an important influence on our ethical thinking.

How would Mill have answered God? The answer seems obvious. "The act of sacrificing my son fails the utilitarian test. The pain exceeds whatever pleasure I might derive from obeying Your command. And even if my delight in serving God is so great that it overwhelms my love of my son, I need to consider my son's and wife's happiness as well." Mill, like Kant, would thus be forced to reject God's command.

The power and purpose of the test reside precisely in its radical demand. A demand inconsistent with our most fundamental human understanding of morality. Fackenheim (1973, p. 54) makes the identical point.

> What lends this pivotal position to the *akedah?* Unquestionably, it is its radicalism. If any human-divine relation is purely religious, it is that of sacrifice. If any sacrifice is total, it is that of life itself. And if any such sacrifice ever runs counter to morality under all circumstances, it is when the life in question is not one's own, or even that of another (possibly consenting) adult, but rather the life of an innocent, helpless, choiceless child. Moreover—if one can speak of "better" and "worse" where only horror seems appropriate—the case is, in at least one sense, worse when the child is one's own, that is, when one acts as though to be a parent is to be an owner.

And yet, Abraham accepts God's command.

Abraham's insight and behavior at the *akedah* represent the core idea of monotheism, and thus Judaism. For millennia, Jews have referred to the memory of this episode as constituting the foundation of our relationship with God. This point is so obvious that one example suffices. On Rosh Hashanah, at the very climax of the Musaf (additional) service (Birnbaum 1951, p. 342), Jews pray as follows:

> Our God and God of our fathers, remember us favorably and visit us with merciful deliverance from the eternal high heavens. Remember in our favor, Lord our God, the covenant, the kindness, and solemn promise which thou didst make to our father Abraham on Mount Moriah; be mindful of the time when our father Abraham bound his son Isaac on the altar, suppressing his compassion that he might do thy will wholeheartedly. May thy mercy likewise hold back thy anger from us; in thy great goodness, may thy wrath turn away from thy people, thy city, thy land, thy heritage.

We, therefore, must follow Fackenheim's suggestion (1973, p. 54) in reference to this narrative. "Only horror is appropriate, humanly and morally. Yet religiously we cannot cut off further questioning, lest we shun prematurely dark possibilities to which openness is a philosophical requirement."

Abraham's insight, in "suppressing his compassion," is that human morality itself is contingent. It is contingent not on thought and understanding, but on a commanding God. If God does not command, then ultimately man has no responsibilities other than those he invents for himself. Unless morality is viewed in the context of God, it is anchorless. Ultimately, Abraham teaches us, we choose morality because of our love of God.

The Bible and Jewish tradition do not completely dismiss a rule-based morality. In fact, the tannaitic sage Hillel summarizes biblical teaching with the terse rule, "Whatever is hateful to thee, do it not unto thy fellow" (Shabbat 31a). Hillel's dictum is directly derived from Leviticus 19:18. The Torah writes: "Love thy neighbor as yourself." Most importantly, however, the verse does not end here. The final phrase of the commandment is: "I am the Lord." This is precisely what is meant by viewing "morality in the context of God." The Torah agrees that one must love one's neighbor. This command is distinct from the Torah's command to love God. ("And thou shalt love the Lord thy God with all thy heart, and with all thy soul, and with all thy might" [Deuteronomy 6:5].) Nevertheless, the command to love one's neighbor is contingent on our love of God. It is because we love God that we accept an obligation to love our fellow man, and not vice-versa.

If Abraham believes in God, he has no choice. God is the source of his ethical obligation. Whatever God commands, man must obey. No matter how extreme, no matter how radical the sacrifice, Abraham must choose God. The view expressed here is consistent with Rabbi Joseph Soloveitchik's view (as presented by Peli 1980):

> Only when man has one king, to whom he owes allegiance and absolute loyalty, can he be considered a liberated and free person. Subjugation to anyone else borders on idolatry. People subjugate themselves in many ways. What can be better or more desirable than binding oneself to one's family and children. The Torah teaches us to love and cherish our children and brings as an example, "as a father takes pity over his children." *At the very same time, the story of the Binding of Isaac is perhaps there to teach us that parental love must not be transformed into absolute bondage, which has idolatrous connotations* [emphasis added].

Pushed to the wall, Abraham recognized that if he chose a human morality over God's command, he would be left with nothing. Human morality without God's sanction is no morality. It is a tower of Babel made of brick for stone and slime for mortar. We can now answer the question with which we began, why such an extreme test? Why does God require Abraham to sacrifice his son? The lesson must be unambiguous, as Rashi and the Midrash make plain in the following comment from God to Abraham, [Genesis 22:12] "For now I have a reply to give Satan and to the nations who wonder at the love I bear you . . . now that they see that you are in awe of God." God has given Abraham an absolutely unequivocal opportunity to demonstrate his priorities. God first. Any less extreme formulation of the test would have left Satan with an opening.

The rabbis are unanimous in their endorsement of Abraham's behavior. Even so, the following midrashic comment [Genesis 22:13] suggests a warning: *"Lay not thine hand upon the lad to slay him* [Genesis 22:12]. Then he [Abraham] said to God, `If this be so I have come here for nothing; let me at least inflict a wound on him and draw some blood from him.'" This is a strange rabbinic embellishment. The ordeal is seemingly over. The angel of God has explicitly stated, "Lay not thine hand upon the lad." And yet the midrash suggests that Abraham might want to "at least inflict a wound" so as to avoid a purposeless mission.

Perhaps the midrash is recognizing an inherent danger of Abraham's and therefore monotheism's claim. Those who desire to obey God's command at all costs are often carried away by their own passion, desire, and blindness. Abraham is so God intoxicated that even after the test is formally over, he still wants to demonstrate his deep love for God. The midrash concludes by having God state, "Neither do thou anything to him—inflict no blemish on him." God Himself reminds Abraham that He already has sufficient proof of Abraham's total devotion. But again, it must be emphasized, this danger—real as it is—in no way softens the primary meaning of the *akedah*. Abraham ultimately has no choice but to obey God's commandment. As this narrative establishes, Jewish ethics begins with the acknowledgment of God as the ultimate source of value.

The Centrality of Community

A second characteristic distinguishing the substance of Jewish ethics from philosophical approaches is the centrality of community. If Jewish ethics is an attempt to answer the question "What does God command us to do?", it necessarily presupposes the existence of community. God's religious and ethical commandments are directed first to the community and only afterward to individual members of the community. As Rabbi Joseph Soloveitchik has perceptively noted, the individual as an individual can make no claim on God, "he has made no covenant with Him" (quoted in Peli 1980, p. 129). When one accepts the Jewish covenant, one enters only as a member of the Jewish community.

Christian thinkers have carefully considered some of the implications of a religiously based ethics focusing on the centrality of community. A Jewish business ethics can easily endorse the view of Paul Camenisch (1986, p. 437). Writing in the *Journal of Business Ethics* about the foundation of a religiously based business ethics, he said:

> Where then would I start? With a single indispensable assertion about the nature of religious ethics, that religious/ theological ethics always recognizes and struggles to stay true to the fact that morality—whether religious, simply human, or whatever—is not an abstract creation of reflective mind, or an intellectual exercise in manipulating concepts, but is at its very root and heart a *community*, a *"lived"*, or... an *embodied* reality. It tries to remain true to its conviction that morality is an activity, or, better still, a dimension of many activities of *persons* in all their complexity, not just in the "rationality," struggling to live together in *community*. Morality is part of their continuing effort first to make such life together possible at all, and then to further humanize that shared experience.

Camenish correctly concludes the discussion by observing an important implication. "Religious ethics always has at least one eye on the implications for the community, on the needs of the community for the sake of which those activities are undertaken" (p. 437).

Dennis McCann (1986, p. 447), in the same issue of the *Journal of Business Ethics*, clarifies:

In particular, precisely because theological ethics is inevitably constituted in a hermeneutic relationship to a community and an ethos that antedate the historic formation of modernity, it tends to mediate moral perspectives that provide critical leverage against the pervasive dominance of bureaucratic modes of rationality and social organization. These perspectives, I contend, may be a potent weapon in our common struggle to exorcise the Myth of Amoral Business.

In other words, McCann believes that the centrality of community in religious business ethics serves to mitigate problems associated with the dominant view in our culture, which accepts the idea of business as a value-free enterprise. The religious focus on community is in contrast to philosophical approaches that tend to view ethics as a problem faced by the isolated individual. (See also Leahy 1986 and Krueger 1986.)

Consider the following two cases:

1. In 1992, shortly after the Los Angeles riots, Time Warner Corporation released an album in which the rapper Ice-T "exhorted listeners to murder police" (Wood 1994, p. 260). *Body Count*, the title of the album, was released with an advisory warning label to parents. Time Warner defended its decision by noting the corporation's responsibility to protect the individual artist's freedom of expression. From the religious view, a perspective in which men and women view themselves first as members of communities, Time Warner's decision is highly questionable. Executives, board members, and the corporation itself are part of the community, and as such have responsibilities to maintain the community.

2. During the 1960s and 1970s, multinational corporations began to market infant formula in developing countries. As summarized by Wood (1994),

Depending on their own expertise, companies chose one of two basic avenues for marketing infant formula. Most

formula firms, including Nestlé, were primarily food manu-
facturers. They preferred to use direct mass media and bill-
board consumer advertising and face-to-face sales efforts.
Ads showed pictures of beautiful, bottle-fed babies and
their beautiful, happy mothers. In addition, point-of-sale
sampling was a popular marketing tactic, and free samples
were routinely made available to new mothers in hospitals
and clinics.

This marketing strategy came under intense ethical scrutiny.
The attack centered on the accusation that mothers in developing
countries were too poor to afford enough formula and did not
fully understand how to use it properly. Thus bottle-fed babies
were not receiving proper nutritional requirements. It is not at all
surprising that religious groups such as the Infant Formula Action Committee and the Interfaith Council on Corporate Responsibility were among the most vocal opponents of the marketing
strategy. A religiously based ethics centered on community cannot sanction an economic strategy, even a profitable one, which
does not recognize the unique characteristics of the community.

Turning to Jewish texts, three distinct talmudic principles can
be understood in the context of promoting the creation, maintenance, and enhancement of community. Each of these principles
has important implications for a Jewish business ethics.

First, Judaism recognizes different levels of responsibility to
those in need. Interpreting the biblical obligation to lend funds to
the needy (Exodus 22:24), the Talmud concludes that one has a
primary obligation to meet the legitimate financial needs of the
members of one's own family. Only after satisfying family needs
does one have an obligation to meet the needs of residents of
one's city. Finally, after satisfying the needs of one's city, only
then does one have an obligation to meet the needs of people in
other towns (Bava Metzia 71a).

It is difficult to defend a hierarchy of this kind from a purely
philosophical perspective. An impartial philosopher, taking in
the "view from nowhere," as Thomas Nagel (1986) aptly put it,

would not recognize the needs of one's own city or even one's own family as being special. Philosophers would more likely conclude that all the poor should be treated alike. Yet, if one begins with the idea of community (as in Jewish ethics), and the centrality of family within the community, special responsibilities can be more easily defended. In fact, it can be argued that the very existence of families and local communities is dependent on one's meeting the special responsibilities demanded by these institutions. A family in which a sister neglected the legitimate needs of her brother would hardly be a model family.

If it is true that local communities demand special responsibilities, an important implication for business ethics emerges. Businesses engaged in philanthropic activities should meet the needs of those closest to the business enterprise first. Meeting the needs of its employees and of residents of the communities in which it operates would have strong justification from a Jewish perspective.

An excellent example is AT&T's decision to promote community day care. Although corporate charitable giving is often difficult to defend (what right do managers have to spend shareholders' money?), some philanthropic activities are arguably more legitimate than others. Perhaps this point can best be illustrated by examining AT&T's initiative on neighborhood day care centers for young children. At the urging of the philanthropic foundation, AT&T's human services division created a special fund that supports expanded day care in company neighborhoods.

This project has strong justification. First, AT&T, and in particular the human services division, is familiar with the day care problems faced by its predominantly female work force. AT&T needs to attract motivated workers. To do so, the company needs to provide a convenient place to work. Enhancing the availability and quality of day care is an important step in this direction. Second, although no one would charge that AT&T is directly responsible for the difficulties faced by working parents, the company is well aware that those parents who choose to work for it are in need of some kind of day care solution. The mere existence of this knowledge alone may constitute a certain level of responsibility. Third, and most importantly for our present purposes, there exists a high degree of consensus among corporate stakeholders. Consistent with the talmudic conception of charity, the initiative is designed to meet the needs of those closest to the business enterprise.

> Employees benefit: The employee union at AT&T made it plain that family care should be included as part of the employee benefits package.
> Residents of local communities benefit: Residents enjoy better access to quality day care.
> Managers benefit: Managers can attract employees from a wider pool of job applicants.
> Shareholders benefit: To the extent that better-qualified employees can sustain and generate higher profit levels, shareholders will earn higher rates of return.

AT&T's day care initiative thus seems to qualify as a legitimate form of corporate philanthropy.

A second principle of talmudic law designed to promote communal well-being is known as *kofin al midat s'dom,* which is usually translated as "one is compelled not to act in the manner of Sodom." Shmuel Shilo (1980, p. 49) interprets the principle as follows: "If A has a legal right and the infringement of such right by B will cause no loss to A but will remove some harm from, or bring a benefit to B, then the infringement of A's right will be allowed." In other words, talmudic law, by invoking the *kofin* principle, can compel A to surrender a legal right in order to improve B's lot, assuming no cost to A. Shilo (p. 77) further elaborates:

> *Kofin al midat S'dom* is a legal principle of very wide application. It is founded on a theory—not surprising for a legal system based on religious law which abounds with moral and equitable commands—that even where one does

not have a legal right he can acquire one on the basis of *kofin*. Looking at this from the standpoint of the subservient party, the *kofin* rule overrides one's legal rights where insisting on exercising them brings him no benefit and waiving them in a specific situation would be beneficial to another. . . . *Kofin* is almost all-encompassing. It can alter contractual obligations; it can be applied not only to allay a possible damage but also to allow for a benefit or even a monetary profit; real property of another can be impinged on and there even is a minority view that another's property may be occupied against the owner's will.

The principle of *kofin* is unanimously accepted in Jewish law. What is controversial, however, is the extent of its application. The most difficult question arises in defining the meaning of cost. Jewish legal precedents demonstrate that economic costs are not all treated alike. The talmudic cases cited in Bava Batra (12b) and Ketubot clarify:

A certain man bought a field adjacent to the estate of his father-in-law. When they came to divide the latter's estate, he said: Give me my share next to my own field. [The usual manner of dividing such property was by lot.] Rabbah said: This is a case where a man can be compelled not to act after the manner of Sodom (*kofin al midat s'dom*). R. Joseph strongly objected to this, on the ground that the brothers can say to him: We reckon this field as specially valuable like the property of the family of Mar Marion. The law follows R. Joseph.

The plaintiff's claim in this case, as the text makes plain, is *kofin*. The specifics are as follows: The plaintiff argues that all the fields constituting the original estate are of equal market value, i.e., if one were to sell them, the selling prices of the fields would be identical. On this basis, the plaintiff asks the court to force the brothers to give up their legal right to the lottery. The plaintiff reasons that his brothers incur no cost in waiving the lottery, but he will benefit as a result of obtaining a field adjacent to his first field. (It is taken as self-evident that two adjacent fields are more valuable than two nonadjacent fields.) While Rabbah accepts this claim, R. Joseph denies it. However, R. Joseph denies it not because he does not accept the *kofin* principle, but because he does not accept the assumption that the original fields were of equal market value. He explicitly states that the field in question "is specially valuable," and presumably could be sold for a higher price than the nonadjacent fields. Based on the specifics of R. Joseph's denial, it is clear that had the plaintiff's original fact assessment been accurate, i.e., had all the fields been of equal market value, then even he would have agreed with the plaintiff and Rabbah. In fact, as the talmudic discussion unfolds, in a similar case where indeed the fields in question are of equal market value, R. Joseph himself concludes, "We do compel a man not to act in the manner of Sodom" (Bava Batra 12b). Once again, the Talmud asserts, the law follows R. Joseph.

R. Asher b. Yehiel (1250–1327, Germany, Spain), known as the Rosh, perceptively noted an important implication of the *kofin* principle as applied in this and other talmudic cases. R. Asher's interpretation dramatically widens the scope of the *kofin* principle. On the face of it, the case under discussion seems noncontroversial. If there exists an established market value for the fields, and the fields are of equal value, the brothers incur no loss, and the plaintiff gains by dint of inheriting the adjacent field. In other words, A, in giving up his legal entitlement to the lottery, incurs no loss, while B gains. Later rabbinic authorities, however, questioned this interpretation. This view, propounded by R. Jacob Tam (1110–1171, France) and the leading French school of commentators, the tosafists, suggests that surely there is a loss for the brothers. The brothers could argue that the plaintiff himself would be willing to pay them a premium for this particular field precisely because he already owns the adjacent one. Thus, the *kofin* principle is inapplicable here. If the court forces the brothers to waive the lottery, it is imposing an opportunity cost on them. R.

Asher b. Yehiel disagrees with this theory. He notes that if this interpretation is correct, it would nullify the *kofin* principle outright. In any conceivable case where B stands to gain, A could always argue that B would be willing to pay a premium above the market value. According to R. Asher's reading, to retain the force of the *kofin* principle, it must follow that the cost to A of forfeiting his ability to negotiate a premium from B over and above the market price—because of B's unique circumstances as owner of the adjacent field—is not considered a cost when applying *kofin*.

R. Asher's reading of the *kofin* principle underscores its fundamental substance as a legal and ethical principle. It also fits well with the talmudic material. The following case from the talmudic tractate of Ketubot (103a) illustrates the far-reaching implications.

> A certain man once leased his mill to another in [consideration of the latter's services in] grinding [his corn]. Eventually he [the former] became rich and bought another mill and an ass. Thereupon he said to the other, "Until now I have had my grinding done at your place, but now pay me rent."

The Talmud concludes: "If he [the lessee] has [sufficient orders for] grinding at his mill, he may, in such circumstances, be compelled [not to act] in the manner of Sodom."

In this case, the lessor can successfully argue, on the basis of *kofin*, for a change in the terms of the existing contract. The lessee is forced to give up the legal rights that would normally (in the absence of *kofin*) inhere in the contract. The lessee, released from his obligation to grind the lessor's corn, is required by the *kofin* principle to take on an additional customer. (It is only under the explicit assumption of "sufficient orders" that the *kofin* principle is applicable.) With the proceeds the lessee obtains from the new customer he pays cash, rather than services, to the lessor. The lessee incurs no additional cost, and the lessor benefits by grinding his own corn and receiving rent in the form of cash payments. It should be observed that the lessee in this case, as above, according to R. Asher's reading, is prohibited from negotiating a premium from the lessor for his willingness to change the terms of the contract. It can be argued that if the lessor potentially benefits by changing the terms of the contract, the lessee potentially incurs a cost. This cost, however, is a direct function of the unique circumstances of the lessor and is therefore ruled out. Presumably, in the absence of knowledge about the lessor's new mill, the lessee would be indifferent between paying cash and continuing the terms of the original agreement.

The key to understanding these talmudic cases is the idea that the defendants are not able to negotiate and capture payments based on circumstances unique to the plaintiffs. In the case of the fields, the brothers are not allowed to extract a premium for waiving their rights to a lottery. The value of the lottery is derived solely from the fact that their brother happens to already own a field adjoining the property in question. In the case of the mill, the value of the existing contract is derived solely from the fact that the lessor purchased a second mill. In the absence of the *kofin* principle, the defendants would be able to extract some payments from the plaintiffs, depending on the relative negotiating skills of the parties involved.

The logic of the *kofin* principle is community welfare. If the plaintiff could not rely on the *kofin* principle, he would potentially be forced into a costly negotiation process. This could only result in a mere transfer of wealth from one party to another. The community as a whole would be worse off to the extent that the negotiation process is assumed to have some positive cost. The assumption of costly negotiations is well warranted. If this analysis is correct, it presumably follows, therefore, that if the defendant could show that in the absence of exercising his legal right the community as a whole would be worse off (and not just the defendant), the *kofin* principle would be ineffective.

This last point apparently drives the following legal decision of Rabbi Ezekiel Landau (1713–1793, Bohemia). The facts of the case are as follows. The owner of a field close to a source of water dug an irrigation ditch on his own property. The owner of the adjacent field argues that he should be allowed to extend the irrigation ditch, with no payment to the first party, so as to allow the water to flow to his own property. The basis for the claim is the *kofin* principle. The owner of the first field incurs no additional cost, and the owner of the second field stands to benefit. In this case, however, Rabbi Landau cogently argues that the *kofin* principle is inappropriate. The owner of the first field can legitimately threaten to refill the irrigation ditch unless compensation is made to him. This case is distinct from the cases analyzed above in that if the law does not protect the property rights of the owner of the first field, the community as a whole will ultimately be worse off. If one cannot reasonably expect payment for one's labor (digging the original ditch), individual members of the community will rationally choose to dig fewer ditches. In this sense, the communal welfare is decreased.

To summarize thus far, the *kofin* principle is universally accepted in Jewish sources as a legal and ethical principle. The principle states that if B potentially benefits, under certain circumstances, the court can compel A to waive some of his legal rights (assuming no cost to A). Further, at least according to one interpretation, A cannot use the argument that if there is a benefit to B (based on the unique circumstances of B), B should be willing to pay a premium to him. The last case cited above, however, illustrates that if the community as a whole will ultimately suffer from the application of *kofin*, A is allowed to negotiate a payment from B.

The *kofin* principle has clear implications in a modern economy. Consider the following sample case (Kahneman, Knetsch, and Thaler 1986, p. 735):

> A landlord rents out a small house. When the lease is due for renewal, the landlord learns that the tenant has taken a job very close to the house and is therefore unlikely to move. The landlord raises the rent $40 per month more than he was planning to.

The vast majority of respondents to a national survey, when asked to rate this decision in terms of fairness, stated that they thought it was an unfair business practice. From a purely free-market perspective, these responses are difficult to interpret. In a free market, the landlord can charge whatever price he desires. However, if we assume an intuitive acceptance of a *kofin*-like principle among respondents, the responses are readily understandable. The tenant can argue, at least from an ethical standpoint if not from a legal perspective, that the landlord should willingly waive his legal right to increase the monthly rental payments. There is no cost to the landlord and the tenant will gain. The landlord's potential counterclaim that there is a cost, a $40 cost, is rejected. Under *kofin*, the landlord cannot negotiate a premium from the tenant based on a unique circumstance of the tenant. In this case, the unique circumstance is the tenant's acceptance of a job near the house. Respondents who rate the landlord's decision as unfair must be assuming that the market value of the rental unit—i.e., the price which the landlord could reasonably expect to obtain from other prospective tenants—is the original rent. This reading is a reasonable one given that the case states that the landlord chooses to raise the rent only after learning that the tenant has accepted a new job. If the landlord successfully negotiates his rental increase, the community as a whole is no better off, and is in fact worse off, due to the costs of negotiation and ill-will created as a result of the decision.

The *kofin* principle would also seem to have important implications in terms of employer-employee relationships. The following case illustrates a potentially important application.

A business enterprise owns and operates five profitable factories in five different regions of the country. All factory employees earn $10 per hour. Management believes that, although it would need to pay replacement workers at least $10 per hour, a credible threat to lay off current employees would force them to accept a $1 per hour pay cut. Management's strategy is based on the realistic assumption that current employees would accept a small pay cut rather than incur the costs associated with the time and uncertainty of searching for a new job. Employees may correctly conclude that they cannot afford to be out of a job even for a short period of time. In order to strengthen the threat, management terminates employees at one of its factories. Management is willing to forgo profits from one of the five factories because the potential savings resulting from the pay cut at the remaining four factories will more than offset the lost profits.

It would seem that management's decision to close a profitable factory is unfair. But why? Does not management have the legal right to close factories? Once again, the answer seems to be a general acceptance, if only at the level of intuition, of a *kofin*-like principle. From an ethical standpoint, employees at the closed factory can claim *kofin*. Although the employees recognize management's legal right to close the factory, they can potentially argue that management incurs no additional cost by waiving its closure rights, and they will benefit. Management's potential counterclaim that it incurs a cost to the extent that it cannot credibly negotiate a wage reduction with the remaining factory employees is not allowed. Under *kofin*, management cannot negotiate wages based solely on the unique circumstances of the employees. Here, the unique circumstances are the transaction costs, in time and uncertainty, that the employees must incur to obtain new jobs at $10 per hour. It turns out, under *kofin*, that management must pay employees the same hourly wages it would pay replacement workers. (Obviously, if management can show that replacement workers would be willing to work for $9 per hour, *kofin* would not apply.) In this case, as in all *kofin* cases, the critical issue is the welfare of the community as a whole. In this case, the costs associated with the negotiation process might be extremely high. In addition to the time and ill-will, employees might certainly contemplate a work stoppage or a strike. With the acceptance of *kofin*, communal welfare is ultimately enhanced.

As noted above, the *kofin* principle is a legal principle of very wide application. However, the Talmud itself recognizes the limitations of relying exclusively on legal rules. The following case (Kahneman, Knetsch, and Thaler 1986) illustrates the weakness of relying solely on the law.

A small photocopying shop has one employee who has worked in the shop for six months and earns $9 per hour. Business continues to be satisfactory, but a factory in the area has closed and unemployment has increased. Other small shops have now hired reliable workers at $7 an hour to perform jobs similar to those done by the photocopy shop employee. The owner of the shop reduces the employee's wage to $7.

In this example, we assume that the law allows for the renegotiation of the wages. Further, it is clear, that here *kofin* is inapplicable. The owner of the photocopying shop could hire a replacement worker at $7 per hour. Therefore, the employee cannot claim that there is no cost to the owner, or that the cost is related to his unique circumstances. Nevertheless, once again, the vast majority of respondents to a national survey rated this as an unfair business practice. The talmudic principle of *lifnim mishurat hadin,* usually translated as "beyond the letter of the law," is applicable here. This principle requires one to waive legal rights, even if it means incurring some cost, in order to meet ethical obligations. Nahmanides (1194–1270, Spain), who described an individual who exploited the limitations of the law as a "scoundrel within the law," provides a classical description of the principle (quoted by Lichtenstein 1978, p. 108).

> For it is impossible to mention in the Torah all of a person's actions toward his neighbors and acquaintances, all of his commercial activity, and all social and political institutions. So after He had mentioned many of them such as, "Thou shalt not go about as a tale-bearer," "Thou shalt not stand by idly by the blood of thy fellow," "Thou shalt not curse the deaf," "Thou shalt rise up before age," and the like, the Torah resumes to say generally that one should do the good and the right in all matters, to the point that there are included in this compromise, *lifnim mishurat hadin* . . .

The principle of *lifnim mishurat hadin* is extremely relevant for a Jewish business ethics. Its implications are discussed fully in chapter 6. At this point, we simply note that Jewish law itself recognizes its own inherent limitations and the need to incorporate ethical language. The owner of the photocopying shop, viewing the decision strictly in legal terms, faces no obstacles in reducing the wages. Nevertheless, the employee may indeed have an ethical claim, assuming that he or she has been instrumental in maintaining the profitable activities of the shop. Perhaps the employee, by virtue of time invested in the shop and effective labor performed, has earned a "stake" in the business.

Religious ethics, and Jewish ethics in particular, stresses the importance of community. Three specific talmudic principles reflect this idea. First, the recognition of different levels of responsibility for charitable giving (Bava Metzia 71a) is a bedrock concept. Without some notion of different levels of responsibility, it is almost impossible to imagine the existence of communities. Second, the *kofin* principle recognizes and formalizes a minimum standard. If B's situation can be improved at no cost to A, A should willingly waive legal rights. Third, *lifnim mishurat hadin* is a principle that establishes the need to incorporate ethical language beyond legal rules. Jewish texts recognize the existence of "scoundrels within the law." Where *kofin* is a minimal standard, *lifnim mishurat hadin* is much more demanding. The creation, maintenance, and enhancement of community demand all three principles.

Even recognizing the importance of community from a Jewish perspective, the idea of community has its darker side. The misapplication of a communitarian spirit can lead to xenophobia, fear of the outsider. A community must be constantly on guard against the inherent tendency to create a community of "identical" members. The Talmud warns us about the Sodomite practice of providing a standard-size bed to visitors. "If the guest was too long, they shortened him [by lopping off his feet]; if too short, they stretched him out" (Sanhedrin 109b). By stressing the importance of community, one automatically is tempted to mistreat nonmembers of the community. Therefore, an ethics focusing on community alone is not sufficient. The place of community needs to be understood against the backdrop of God's ultimate authority and viewed in the context of Judaism's insistence that religion is not only about right action, but also provides a vision of what we might become.

The Promise of Transformation

Jewish ethics is defined as the interpretation of the written and oral Torah to determine what God commands us to be and to do. This definition suggests that from a religious perspective the first question in ethics is always about God's values. The definition does not suggest, however, that it is the only question. A third substantive issue where a religious perspective, and more particularly a Jewish perspective, diverges from purely secular approaches is the focus on character as opposed to isolated actions. Ethics, from a religious perspective, is not only about identifying specific rules of behavior. In this sense, the religious enterprise is an ambitious one. From a religious perspective, it is proper and meaningful to ask: What does God want us to be? This question suggests that in its very essence, Judaism promises an individual and a communal transformation. If this is correct, it has important implications for a Jewish business ethics.

Once again, we return to the thought of Rabbi Joseph B. Soloveitchik. In his view, Judaism recognizes two groups of mitzvot (commandments). The first group consists of those commandments in which the performance (the act of performing the specific mitzvah) is identical with its fulfillment. Rabbi Soloveitchik provides the example of taking the four species on the Feast of Tabernacles (Sukkot). The biblical mandate (Leviticus 23:40) specifically states, "And ye shall take you . . . the fruit of goodly trees, branches of palm trees . . ."). According to Rabbi Soloveitchik, the wording of the biblical verse indicates that the mitzvah is completely fulfilled by the performance. He explains, however (as quoted by Peli 1980, p. 80), that there is a second group of commandments in which performance and fulfillment are distinct.

But there are other precepts whose performance and fulfillment are not identical, for example when the performance of the precept is through specific action of some kind, or through a verbal utterance, but its fulfillment is up to the heart. The precept is, in fact, performed by means of an utterance or an external act, but fulfillment is dependant on attaining a certain degree of spiritual awareness.

The mitzvot in this second group demand both action and a spiritual transformation. Among the most important examples Rabbi Soloveitchik cites is the daily requirement to recite the Sh'ma. Its real fulfillment is not in formally rehearsing the verbal formulation, "Hear, O Israel, the Lord is our God, the Lord is one," but "depends upon the acceptance of the yoke of the heavenly Kingdom" (Peli 1980, p. 81). These commandments demand right action and right intention.

When Rabbi Soloveitchik applies this idea to the overarching Jewish call for repentance (teshuvah), its full implications become apparent. Repentance, and more generally Jewish ethics as a whole, is not only about altering our actions; more importantly, it is traditionally understood as a kind of personal transformation. In describing the teshuvah process, Rabbi Soloveitchik (as quoted by Peli 1980, pp. 84–85) writes:

> It is a precept whose essence is not in the performance of certain acts or deeds, but rather in a process that at times extends over a whole lifetime, a process that begins with remorse, with a sense of guilt, with man's increasing awareness that there is no purpose to his life, with a feeling of isolation, of being lost and adrift in a vacuum, of spiritual bankruptcy, of frustration and failure—and the road one travels is very long, until the goal of repentance is actually achieved. Repentance is not a function of a single, decisive act, but grows and gains in size slowly and gradually, until the pentitent undergoes a complete metamorphosis, and then, after becoming a new person, and only then, does repentance take place.

Ideally, the mitzvah of teshuvah is only fulfilled after one becomes "a new person." Like the patriarch Jacob, we must all "strive with God and with men" (Genesis 23:29) to transform ourselves.

The transformation which Rabbi Soloveitchik talks about is primarily a transformation of the individual. David Hartman (1985, p. 77) notes that this limitation is inherent especially in Rabbi Soloveitchik's *Halakhic Man* (1983).

> It would appear from Soloveitchik's focus on self-creation that the inactivity of halakhic man in the public realm may be overlooked if his spirit of activism focuses upon his personal life. . . . There remains, however, a fundamental question that cannot be ignored. . . . If there is so little empirical evidence that Soloveitchik's halakhic man manifested his creativity in the renewal of society, to what extent can the spirit of the Lithuanian talmudic hall of learning serve as an inspiration in the circumstances of Israel, where the task is to create a total Jewish society on the basis of political independence? Indeed, the same question can be asked with regard to any society that invites Jews to participate in shaping the quality of life of the total society.

The goal of this work, ultimately, is to show how traditional sources can help in understanding a Jewish business ethics. In the preceding chapter, it was argued that a focus on the individual is necessary but not sufficient. If Hartman's criticism of Rabbi Soloveitchik is correct, we must go elsewhere.

Michael Walzer has written cogently about a parallel transformation at the level of the community. In his *Exodus and Revolution,* he explores a key theme in the biblical narrative. According to Walzer (1985, pp. 11–12), the biblical material is ultimately and uniquely about the transformation of a whole people.

> For the movement from beginning to end is the key to the historical importance of the Exodus story. The strength of the narrative is given by the end, though it is also crucial that

the end be present at the beginning, as an aspiration, a hope, a promise. What is promised is radically different from what is: the end is nothing like the beginning. This is an obvious but critical point. The Exodus bears no resemblance to those ancient tales of voyages and journeys that, whatever the adventures they include, begin and end at home. It's not like the journey of the eleventh-century Egyptian priest Wen-Amon to Byblos in Phoenicia and then, after many difficulties, back (though the narrative breaks off while he is on his way) to his temple at Karnak. Nor can it be described as an odyssey, a long wandering such as Homer recounted, at the end of which wait wife and child (and ancient servant and faithful dog). According to the biblical story, only Joseph's bones return to Canaan; for the living Israelites the promised land is a new home, and no one is waiting there to greet them. In the literature of the ancient world only the Aeneid resembles the Exodus in its narrative structure, describing a divinely guided and world-historical journey to something like a promised land. That is why the Aeneid was the only rival of the Exodus in the arguments over the American Great Seal. But Rome, though it represents for Virgil a "new order of the ages," is not, after all, significantly different from Troy; it is only more powerful; while Canaan is the very opposite of Egypt.

The Israelites are thrust out of Egypt. The journey through the wilderness takes 40 years. The congregation, again and again, murmurs against God and Moses. The physical redemption from Egypt proves much easier than the emotional and spiritual redemptions. The congregation enters into a covenant with God. The congregation backslides by creating and worshiping a golden calf that reminds the Israelites of an Egyptian deity. The entire generation must die out. And even Moses himself is not allowed into the Promised Land. Nevertheless, despite the unevenness of the journey, Walzer (1985, p. 12) correctly emphasizes that "the Exodus is a journey forward—not only in time and space. *It is a march toward a goal, a moral progress, a transformation* [emphasis added]."

According to Walzer's reading, the text is not history, but rather has been (and should be) interpreted as a paradigm of political transformation. *Exodus and Revolution* can be read as a kind of modern-day midrashic commentary on the Passover Haggadah's requirement to view ourselves "as if" we had participated in the historical exodus. Unlike traditional midrash, Walzer concludes his book by explicitly stating the lesson (p. 149):

> So pharaonic oppression, deliverance, Sinai, and Canaan are still with us, powerful memories shaping our perceptions of the political world. The "door of hope" is still open; things are not what they might be—even when what they might be isn't totally different from what they are. This is a central theme in Western thought, always present though elaborated in many different ways. We still believe, or many of us do, what the Exodus first taught, or what it has commonly been taken to teach, about the meaning and possibility of politics and about its proper form:
>
> —first, that wherever you live, it is probably Egypt;
>
> —second, that there is a better place, a world more attractive, a promised land;
>
> —and third, that "the way to the land is through the wilderness." There is no way to get from here to there except by joining together and marching.

Rabbi Soloveitchik noted, at the level of the individual, that Jewish ethics is about transformation. One need not accept the status quo as binding. Yesterday has no moral claim on today. Similarly, Walzer notes, at the political level, that the exodus narrative is also about transformation. For Walzer, the community as a whole dare not accept the status quo as binding. "There is a better place . . . a promised land."

The possibility of transformation is inherently hopeful, optimistic, and ambitious. But is it relevant to invoke the imagery of transformation in a discussion of business ethics?

There are two interpretive stances.

The first would emphasize the fact that business is a unique enterprise. Business, according to the first interpretation, is defined as the pursuit of profits. The sole legitimate goal of the business enterprise is maximization of profits. Or, the essence of business is profits. Given the reality of competitive environments, any company which wrongly and naively chooses ethical goals will be soon be eliminated through bankruptcy. A sophisticated version of this argument has been articulated by George J. Benston (1982), among others.[1]

This view would insist on a literalist reading of Rabbi Soloveitchik and other traditional Jewish sources. Hartman's criticism, cited above, about the "inactivity of halakhic man in the public realm" is rejected. Hartman is wrong in assuming that this is a valid critique. The inactivity of halakhic man in the public realm is not a missing element in Soloveitchik's overall philosophy, but rather represents a valid and traditional interpretation of Jewish teachings. This view has a ready answer to the question of why there are relatively few Jewish texts dealing with organizational ethics. Organizational ethics is a nonissue. The first interpretive stance would conclude that transformation and renewal are concepts uniquely applicable to the individual; and thus it is inappropriate to invoke the imagery of transformation in a discussion of business ethics.

By contrast, the second interpretive stance insists that the promise of transformation permeates all aspects of our lives, private and public. It is a religious ideal to be pursued both at the level of the individual and in the context of communal activities, including business. There is no inherent contradiction between Rabbi Soloveitchik's view and Walzer's view. Men and women can re-create themselves and can simultaneously refashion the society we inhabit. Indeed, not only is there no contradiction, but each view reinforces the other. A living community committed to the ideal of ethical improvement at the level of the individual cannot for long ignore the call for ethical improvement in its powerful organizations and institutions. Similarly, a community committed to the ideal of political transformation cannot ignore the need for individual renewal. Individual and societal transformation are two sides of the same coin.

The most important implication of this interpretation is that it now makes sense to step back and ask ourselves what is the truest and best goal of the business enterprise. To suggest that the competitive "realities" of business force us to accept the belief that the sole legitimate goal of business is profit maximization is to deny the possibility of transformation. If there are few texts that focus on business ethics at the level of the organization, in a sense, that is our interpretive choice.

Ultimately, no one individual can choose between the two stances described above. The Jewish community as a whole must choose. The first stance, while perhaps consistent with many traditional teachings, provides an incomplete story. The second stance, with its dual promise of a better place (for the individual and society), is consistent with a greater variety of traditional sources. Most importantly, it provides a complete and convincing vision of the possibility for moral and ethical improvement.

Conclusion

This chapter has argued that Jewish ethics is unique. Specifically, Jewish ethics recognizes God as the ultimate source of value, acknowledges the centrality of the community, and holds out the promise that men and women (living in community) can transform themselves. Each of these elements deals with the substance of Jewish ethics. In the next chapter, we turn our focus to the method of Jewish business ethics.

---

[1] (See page 109) Benston explicitly asserted that consumers, shareholders, and management demonstrate little or no demand for socially responsible activities. Under these restrictive assumptions, Benston builds a strong analytical case suggesting the impossibility of socially responsible activities. He lists four general reasons why managers are limited in terms of choices: the market for goods and services, the markets for finance and for corporate control, the market for managerial services, and finally, internal and external monitoring systems.

Given that Benston's consumers are "rarely interested" in corporate social responsibility activities, the market for goods and services serves to constrain managerial decisions. Managers are unable to expend additional resources on environmental projects and pass along the costs of the these activities to consumers. Consumers simply will not pay more to help defray the costs of environmental clean-up.

Similarly, since shareholders put no value on socially responsible activities, the markets for finance and corporate control also limit the ability of managers to engage in these activities. Benston asserts that the "poor stewardship" associated with decisions to engage in socially responsible activities will inevitably lead to lower share prices. And, in turn, "the decline in the market price of corporations' shares increases the likelihood of a corporate takeover to displace the managers" (p. 91). Therefore, managers concerned about their own jobs have a strong built-in incentive to avoid these activities.

The market for managerial services, like the markets discussed above, also constrains managers. At this point in the argument, Benston equates social responsibility to "self-serving decisions" (p. 91). Thus, the more a manager is perceived as engaging in these activities, the more difficult he or she will find obtaining a new managerial position. In Benston's words, "As is the case in markets generally, other producers as well as consumers have incentive to learn about and provide information on the value of the product" (p. 91). To the extent that a manager is known as a socially responsible manager, his or her value will decline.

Finally, and according to Benston most importantly, the existence of internal and external monitoring systems will prevent managers from "misusing the shareholders' resources" (p. 92). According to Benston, most managers (like consumers and shareholders) have no desire to engage in socially responsible activities. They thus find it in their own interest to set up and design internal and external monitoring systems to attest to the fact that they are not engaging in unprofitable activities. In the absence of external auditors, for example, management's "compensation would be reduced by the amount of resources that they would be expected to divert from the shareholders" (p. 92). Simply put, it is in the interest of managers to hire auditors to attest to the fact that no socially responsible activities have been undertaken.

Benston's conclusion is clearly stated. Managers have little or no discretion to act other than in the interests of shareholders. Since it has been assumed that shareholders have no taste for socially responsible activities, managers cannot and will not engage in these activities.

5

The Method of Jewish Business Ethics: Interpretation

In chapter 3, acceptable goals for a Jewish business ethics were set out. In chapter 4, we questioned briefly the need for a specifically Jewish business ethics. The answer offered was based on a study of the substance of Jewish ethics. Jewish ethics is distinguished from secular approaches in three ways. Jewish ethics recognizes God as the ultimate source of value, acknowledges the centrality of the community, and holds out the promise that men and women (living in community) can transform themselves. By contrast, secular approaches need make no assumptions about the existence or nonexistence of God, generally (although certainly not always) start with the idea of an isolated man or woman as fundamental, and make no a priori claims about man's and the community's unique potential for transformation. Richard De George (1986, p. 424), for example, a contemporary expert on academic business ethics, recently described the secular approach: "The philosopher in business ethics starts from the assumption that he can deal with moral issues in business independently of any consideration of God's existence or of revelation. He attempts to work on the basis of reason and human experience alone."

In this chapter, the discussion turns from issues of substance to issues of methodology. If we claim to be studying Jewish business ethics, what is it that we are doing? How do we proceed? In answering these questions, an important characteristic of religious ethics, and more particularly of Jewish ethics, emerges. The uniqueness of a Jewish business ethics hinges on the method of inquiry as much as on the substance of the inquiry.

Three Paths of Moral Philosophy

Michael Walzer, in his *Interpretation and Social Criticism*, suggests that there are three common and important approaches to moral philosophy. He labels these the path of discovery, the path of invention, and the path of interpretation.

Discovery

Philosophers who walk the path of discovery accept the idea that moral truths exist *out there*, like unexplored continents, patiently awaiting discovery. The task of the philosopher is to step back (or better, to step up), disentangle himself from parochial interests, and describe the newly discovered moral rules. Perched high above the terrain, the moral philosopher sees further than most by dint of the exceptional view. The good news of the discovery is then shared with others. It is a kind of natural revelation, as opposed to a divine one.

Walzer (1987, p. 5) aptly describes the revelatory moment:

> The moral world comes into view as the philosopher steps back in his mind from his social position. He wrenches himself loose from his parochial interests and loyalties; he abandons his own point of view and looks at the world, as Thomas Nagel argues, from "no particular point of view." The project is at least as heroic as climbing the mountain, or marching into the desert. "No particular point of view" is

> somewhere on the way to God's point of view, and what the philosopher sees from there is something like objective value.

The philosopher takes no active part in the creation of the moral world. The philosopher merely reports back on the discovery. His authority rests not on his methods or any special characteristics he may possess, but simply on the fact that he has discovered a real, preexisting truth. Although the discovery cannot be seen or touched, it is as real as any newly found continent.

Those who return from a successful journey of discovery must, of necessity, describe an epochal event. The strength of this path is the insistence on the existence of objective truth. But the claim and content of the discovery can be amazing and unexpected. This is not to suggest that it does not describe a viable path, but at minimum the burden of proof is great. Unlike an explorer returning from a newly discovered continent, the moral philosopher cannot bring back gold or other tangible proofs of the discovery. Precisely because the event of discovery is so unusual, the substance of such modern discoveries tends to be understated. As the importance of the claims grows, the validity of the claims is subject to more and more and scrutiny. If these truths exist out there, how come no one else ever noticed? The more the explorer claims to have discovered, the more the discovery itself is questioned.

An example from the literature of business ethics will clarify. Jensen and Meckling (1994) claim to have made a kind of moral discovery, although it turns out to be mostly negative. With no detectable irony whatsoever, they unveil a "set of characteristics that captures the essence of human nature, but no more" (p. 4). They label their model of human behavior REMM: the Resourceful, Evaluative, Maximizing Model. They describe the process of discovering this model as follows: "REMM is the product of over 200 years of research and debate in economics, the other social sciences, and philosophy. As a result, REMM is now defined in very precise terms" (p. 5). Included among the so-called scientific discoveries is the following "postulate" (p. 5):

REMM is always willing to make trade-offs and substitutions. Each individual is always willing to give up some sufficiently small amount of any particular good (oranges, water, air, housing, honesty, or safety) for some sufficiently large quantity of other goods. Furthermore, valuation is relative in the sense that the value of a unit of any particular good decreases as the individual enjoys more of it relative to other goods.

The most important implication of REMM for our purposes is the following (p. 7):

Like it or not, individuals are willing to sacrifice a little of almost anything we care to name, even reputation or morality, for a sufficiently large quantity of other desired things, and these things do not have to be money or even material goods.

It thus follows that referring to human needs is simply semantic trickery. Therefore, the authors conclude, there really are no housing needs, education needs, food needs, or energy needs. Rather, needs should be exposed for what they are—human desires. Further, given this discovery, it can be shown that employees' values and beliefs can easily be manipulated by changing the corporate reward structure. If certain attitudes, values, and customs are rewarded in the workplace, employees will come to accept them as their own. The authors themselves recognize that not everyone accepts the discovery and its implications. In fact, they write, failure to take the new discovery into account "is one of the most frequent mistakes in the analysis of human behavior" (p. 7).

The point is not to debate the veracity of the claims being made. Simply put, describing Jensen and Meckling's claims as a kind of discovery at least provides the opportunity to pause and view it as a radical departure from the way many people normally think and speak about ethics. The significant point is that

Jensen and Meckling's discovery underscores the position that the responsibility of proof lies with the discoverers. To date, Jensen and Meckling have not offered convincing evidence.

Invention

By contrast, other philosophers have grown weary with the path of discovery. It is as if they have climbed the mountain over and over again only to be perpetually disappointed. If the moral world does not really exist *out there,* then, it is believed, philosophers can invent one.

The path of invention begins in agitation and disappointment. Continual observation has taught that the world we have inherited is deeply flawed. Human beings need ethical laws and a moral vocabulary, and yet it is impossible to find them. The world, as it stands, is morally neutral. In spite of this reality, those who walk the path of invention never lose hope. "They create what God would have created if there were a God" (Walzer 1987, p. 12).

Again, Walzer (1987, p. 9) expands:

> On the other hand, men and women standing nowhere in particular could construct an entirely new moral world— imitating God's creation rather than the discoveries of his servants. They might undertake to do this because they thought that there was no actually existing moral world (because God was dead, or mankind radically alienated from nature, or nature devoid of moral meaning); or they might undertake the construction because they thought that the actually existing moral world was inadequate or that our knowledge of it could never be, as knowledge, sufficiently critical in character.

Walzer continues, "the end is given by the morality we hope to invent. The end is a common life, where justice, or political virtue, or goodness, or some such basic value would be realized" (p. 10).

The key for those engaged in inventing ethical worlds resides in the ground rules of invention. The philosopher's authority can be based on nothing other than the power of his words. Walzer notes that the critical force of the creation is derived solely from the process by which it was created. "If we accept it, it is because we have participated, or can imagine ourselves having participated, in its invention. And if we invent one such principle, we can obviously invent others as we need them" (pp. 12–13).

The great appeal of invention is its insistence on the unique dignity and ability of man. But, as Walzer noted, the authority of all moral inventions is derived from the methodology. One accepts the new morality because one can envision oneself participating in its creation. The weakness inherent in the path of invention, especially in areas of applied ethics, is the usual but rather awkward assumption of consensus at the very moment where disagreement is greatest. The ultimate aim of moral inventors is praiseworthy. However, the process is fraught with difficulties. At the end of the process, we are usually no closer to our goal than at the beginning.

Thomas Donaldson, in *Corporations and Morality* (1982), is interested in "constructing a social contract for business" (p. 36). His work provides a lucid and important example of invention in the context of business ethics. His arguments are well reasoned and carefully couched. He writes that the social contract "is not a typewritten contract in the real world, but a metaphysical abstraction not unlike the `social contract' between citizens and government that philosophers have traditionally discussed" (p. 36). According to Donaldson, such a contract—if it existed—would have concrete significance. It would help us understand the nature of a corporation's indirect obligations. Therefore, the goal of inventing the contract is to clarify the parameters of corporate social responsibility.

Donaldson imagines a primitive society where no productive organizations exist. Building on the terminology of earlier philosophers, he labels this condition the "state of individual production," to distinguish it from the more familiar "state of nature" (p.

44). Specifically, Donaldson's strategy involves:

> 1. Characterizing conditions in a state of individual production (without productive organizations).
> 2. Indicating how certain problems are remedied by the introduction of productive organizations.
> 3. Using the reasons generated in the second step as a basis for specifying a social contract between society and its productive organizations.

In applying this strategy, Donaldson carefully notes the expected benefits and costs associated with the introduction of productive organizations. On the one hand, society will benefit through improved efficiency, stabilized levels of output, and increased income potential. On the other hand, society will also incur additional costs. For example, increased production will lead to a depletion of natural resources and a significant increase in environmental pollution. Further, employees will enjoy less autonomy and control over their work. The contract, according to Donaldson, must specify that the potential benefits outweigh the expected costs. Donaldson summarizes, "the contract specifies that the function of productive organizations is to enhance the welfare of society" (p. 52). This implies that organizations will always be faced with trade-offs. Society cannot expect productive organizations to maximize employee benefits to the exclusion of consumer interests, nor can organizations focus only on consumer demands to the neglect of employee needs.

It would seem, however, that Donaldson's attempt at discovery has not delivered on its original promise of providing an understanding of the corporation's "indirect responsibilities." In fact, somewhat surprisingly, he concludes:

> There is a caveat which has application to the overall contract. People would make a trade-off of the kind just discussed only on the condition that it did not violate certain minimum standards of justice, however these are specified.

... Although the contract might allow productive organizations to undertake actions requiring welfare trade-offs, it
would prohibit organizational acts of injustice.

This conclusion is somewhat disappointing. The contract itself may technically prohibit "acts of injustice." But the contract,
and the process of arriving at the contract, do not specify what
these acts entail. In fact, Donaldson (p. 56) cannot even reject
Friedman's position that the only legitimate goal of the business
organization is profit maximization: "It might even be claimed
that the social contract is best satisfied when business managers
pursue exclusive profit maximization." As with most examples of
discovery, the result is too thin to be of any functional value. If the
original hope was to provide practical guidance in terms of corporate social responsibility, concrete rules with clear implications, one must look elsewhere.

Interpretation

The third path is the path of interpretation. Philosophers need
not and cannot wholly disengage themselves from the world.
This means that it is too late in the game for new discoveries, and
attempts at ethical invention are illusions. Those who walk the
path of interpretation believe that even before they begin the
search, they already live in a moral world. The very process of
searching for moral principles makes sense only if one assumes at
the outset a preexisting morality. Interpreting human institutions
or literary and religious texts requires looking backwards and
seeing where we have been and why we have been there. It is only
in looking backwards and answering these questions that one can
rationally proceed to ask where we should be going. Again,
Walzer (1987, p. 20) is illuminating.

> We do not have to discover the moral world because we
> have always lived there. We do not have to invent it because
> it has already been invented—though not in accordance

with any philosophical method. No design procedure has governed its design, and the result no doubt is disorganized and uncertain. It is also very dense: the moral world has a lived-in quality, like a home occupied by a single family over many generations, with unplanned additions here and there, and all the available space filled with memory-laden objects and artifacts. The whole thing, taken as a whole, lends itself less to abstract modeling than to thick description. Moral argument in such a setting is interpretive in character, closely resembling the work of a lawyer or judge who struggles to find meaning in a morass of conflicting laws and precedents.

Discovery and invention are attempts at escape. The only method that corresponds to our experiences as moral agents is the path of interpretation. As a general description, perhaps Walzer's statement is too far-reaching. But without question, the religious ethicist immediately recognizes as his own Walzer's metaphor of the moral world as a "home occupied by a single family over many generations." Ethical arguments from a Jewish perspective must, of necessity, have a "lived-in quality," and always make reference to and are based on the "memory-laden objects and artifacts."

Walzer's description of the interpretive mode of moral inquiry is consistent with the customary, text-centered, Jewish approach to ethics. The traditionally schooled Jew is not taught to begin anew, as if he or she were to originate the moral discussion, but is educated about what came before. All of us, in a very real sense, are like the potential convert to Judaism in the following talmudic narrative (Shabbat 31a):

> Our rabbis taught: A certain heathen once came before Shammai and asked him, "How many Toroth have you?" "Two," he replied, "the Written Torah and the Oral Torah." "I believe you with respect to the Written, but not with respect to the Oral Torah; make me a proselyte on condition

that you teach me [only] the Written Torah." [But] he [Shammai] scolded and repulsed him as a proselyte. When he went before Hillel, he accepted him as a proselyte. On the first day he taught him *alef, beth, gimmel, dalet,* the following day he reversed [them] to him. "But that is not how you taught them to me yesterday," he protested. "Then you must rely upon me, mustn't you? So rely upon me with respect to the Oral [Torah] too."

The potential convert is initially only willing to accept the authority of the written Torah. Shammai rejects the request, but Hillel embraces the potential convert and begins teaching him the ABC's. Hillel's acceptance of the potential convert is based on his insightful realization that acceptance of any written document as authoritative necessarily implies a prior acceptance of an oral tradition of interpretation. Hillel demonstrates this point to the convert by reversing the ABC's on the second day. The alphabet, the very key to the written Torah, is itself part of the oral Torah. The story demonstrates that in order to read the written text, one must be part of a continuing tradition of interpretation. Hillel's knew that the convert's willingness to accept the written Torah implied a willingness to accept the oral tradition, even if the convert himself had not yet realized this.

Interpretation is what makes traditional approaches traditional. This approach, while less radical than the first two approaches, is hardly passive. Interpretation is not merely a handing down of traditional institutions and texts from one generation to the next. It is the process of taking ownership of the texts, and in turn, the ethical world. Interpretation is thus, in part, a humanly creative process. The rabbinic response to the following difficult passage from Deuteronomy is not unusual. Deuteronomy 22:23–27 states:

If there be a damsel that is a virgin betrothed unto a man, and a man find her in the city, and lie with her; then ye shall bring them both out unto the gate of that city, and ye shall stone them with stones that they die: the damsel, because she cried not, being in the city, and the man, because he hath humbled his neighbor's wife; so thou shalt put away the evil from the midst of thee. But if the man find the damsel that is betrothed in the field, and the man take hold of her, and lie with her; then the man only that lay with her shall die. But unto the damsel thou shalt do nothing; there is in the damsel no sin worthy of death; for as when a man riseth against his neighbor, and slayeth him, even so in this matter. For he found her in the field; the betrothed damsel cried, and there was none to save her.

As the following quotation from the Sifre to Deuteronomy (243) makes plain, the specific wording of these laws troubled the rabbis.

Is it possible that [under all circumstances] in a town she would be liable, while in the country she would be exempt from all liability? Scripture says, "the betrothed damsel cried, and there was none to save her." Lo, if there was someone who might have saved her, whether in town or in the country, she is liable, and if there was no one who might have saved her, whether in town or in the country, she is exempt.

The question which the rabbis posed was deeply puzzling. A woman's guilt or innocence cannot possibly be merely a function of where the event occurred. Yet a plausible reading of the biblical verses might yield just such a conclusion. The rabbis' creative interpretation, grounded in a careful reading of all of the words contained in the verses, leads them in a different direction. By highlighting the fact that the Bible adds seemingly superfluous words to the law, the rabbis are able to carefully reconstruct a better understanding of the law. "The betrothed damsel cried, and there was none to save her." If the location where the event occurred was the law's only concern, these words are unnecessary. The rabbis determined that the purpose of this additional material is not to describe the usual situation in the country, but to prescribe and limit the condition under which the woman—even in the country—would be viewed as innocent. The interpretation of the Sifre quoted above is that only under the assumption that there were no bystanders would the women be deemed innocent. The rabbis extend this logic and apply it to the city as well. Only when there are bystanders would the woman be viewed as guilty. In the absence of bystanders, even in the city, the woman would be deemed innocent. Thus, the rabbinic reading concludes that the key variable is bystanders and not location.

Rabbi Joseph Soloveitchik (1983, pp. 79, 81) explains the Jewish view as follows:

> Halakhic man is a spontaneous, creative type. He is not particularly submissive and retiring, and is not meek when it is a matter of maintaining his own views. Neither modesty nor humility characterizes the image of halakhic man. On the contrary, his most characteristic feature is strength of mind. He does battle for every jot and tittle of the Halakhah, not only motivated by a deep piety but also by a passionate love of the truth. He recognizes no authority other than the authority of the intellect (obviously, in accordance with the principles of tradition). He hates intellectual compromises or fence straddling, intellectual flabbiness, and any type of wavering in matters of law and judgment. This autonomy of the intellect at times reaches heights unimaginable in any other religion. . . .
>
> Halakhic man received the Torah from Sinai not as a simple recipient but as a creator of worlds, as a partner with the Almighty in the act of creation. The power of creative interpretation (*hiddush*) is the very foundation of the received tradition.

Interpretation, according to this view, marries intellectual authority to principles of tradition. This union creates a positive tension, but no inherent contradiction.

Jewish Ethics As Interpretation

A religious approach to business ethics is and must be self-consciously interpretive. The interpretive approach fits with our experience of "doing ethics" and provides a reasonable promise for success. Further, the method of interpretation, in the Jewish context, maintains both the idea of the objectivity of truth and the dignity of man. The interpretive approach sees man as partner. In the secular version, he is a partner with predecessors and colleagues. In the religious version, man is viewed also as a partner with God.

Ronald Dworkin, eminent philosopher of law, has noted (1985, p. 148) that "Propositions of law are not merely descriptive of legal history, in a straightforward way, nor are they simply evaluative in some way divorced from legal history. They are interpretive of legal history, which combines elements of both description and evaluation but is different from both." In his view, interpretation is ultimately not about determining the author's original intention. In many cases, the very idea of intention is not well defined.

But if this view is true, what constitutes interpretation? Dworkin has provided a powerful image capturing the nature of interpretation. Interpreting hard cases at law is like participating in the writing of a chain novel. Each novelist adds a new chapter to an unfinished story. Each contributor is instructed to continue the preexisting novel—never to start out anew.

The specific instructions are twofold. First, the new chapter must "fit" with the previous material. The ultimate goal of the chain novel community is to create a coherent and unified work. "The text provides one severe constraint in the name of identity: all the words must be taken account of and none may be changed to make `it' a putatively better work of art" (Dworkin, p. 150). Second, the new chapter must extend the novel in the best possible way. According to Dworkin, this task requires writers to read the previous material in a way which reveals it as "the best work of art." He writes (p. 158),

> I want to use literary interpretation as a model for the central method of legal analysis. . . . Suppose that a group of novelists is engaged for a particular project and that they draw lots to determine the order of play. The lowest number writes the opening chapter of a novel, which he or she then sends to the next number, who adds a chapter, with the understanding that he is adding a chapter to that novel rather than beginning a new one, and then sends the two chapters to the next number, and so on. Now every novelist but the first has the dual responsibilities of interpreting and creating because each must read all that has gone before in order to establish, in the interpretivist sense, what the novel so far created is.

Dworkin's view of the process or method of determining hard cases at law is particularly useful to help clarify interpretation in the context of Jewish law and ethics (Sacks 1992). The view put forth here is that interpretation understood as a "chain novel" is consistent and complementary with the substance of Jewish ethics as described in the previous chapter. Interpretation, seen as the legitimate method of Jewish ethics, is a path of moral inquiry that promotes the three substantive issues discussed in the last chapter. Although for the purposes of exposition we treat issues of substance separately from methodological issues, these two issues, in essence, cannot easily be separated. The "way" of Jewish ethics is both part of and supports the "what" of Jewish ethics.

God First

In the preceding chapter we argued that Jewish ethics necessarily begins with an understanding of ethics as a response to God's commands. Judaism looks to God as the ultimate source of value in our lives. The Genesis narrative served as an important illustration for this thesis. Interestingly, the image of the chain novel begins with the novelists responding to a set of instructions. Dworkin asks us to suppose that "a group of novelists is engaged for a particular project." The identity of the contractor is suppressed; but it is clear that novelists are not the only actors in the story. In contrast to Dworkin's secular account, we can easily imagine, from a religious perspective, that it is God who engages the "novelists." (This was certainly not Dworkin's intention, but that is beside the point.) Further, a Jewish version of the chain novel image would have God as the author of the first chapter. The first chapter thus constitutes the written Torah. With the completion of the written Torah, man is invited to continue the narrative. Dworkin recognizes that the success of the chain novel image hinges on the assignment "making sense" to the participants. Each novelist in the chain has to understand what he or she is asked to do, and must be committed to the project. The view of God as the initiator of the novel, and the belief that God is the author of the first chapter, provide strong incentives to ensure, from a religious perspective, that Dworkin's own stipulations are met.

Even if we identify God as the originator and author of the first chapter, many readers, unfamiliar with Jewish sources, might question the religious validity of the freedom and creativity inherent in the chain novel image or might doubt its descriptive accuracy. The idea of religious man as both a reader of previous chapters and a writer of his own new chapter is inconsistent, for example, with De George's (1986, p. 425) caricature of religious ethics, which he properly censures.

> The moralistic approach to business consists simply in applying general moral and religious prohibitions or injunctions to the realm of business. It is an old approach to business exemplified in part by philosophers and non-philosophers as well, and in religion it is perhaps more characteristic today of Sunday sermons and of the Moral Majority than of serious contemporary moral theologians.

The moralistic approach, as described by De George, views religious ethics as a process of applying simple rules to simple cases. It is completely devoid of the human element involved in interpretation. It is a straw man created by De George, and is easily and appropriately defeated by him.

Jewish sources are unequivocal in endorsing the view that man has a creative role to play. This idea is best captured by the biblical phrase "It is not in heaven" (Deuteronomy 30:12). The rabbis' interpretation of these words is most famously expressed in the following talmudic tale. Rabbi Eliezer ben Hyrcanus, one of the most important rabbinic scholars in the period after the destruction of the Second Temple, disagreed with the majority of sages about a particular point of law. Rabbi Eliezer declared the oven of Akhnai ritually pure (and thus fit for use), while the sages ruled it impure (and not fit for use). More important than the specific details of this case are the events surrounding its ultimate resolution. After describing the disagreement, the Talmud continues (Bava Metzia 59b):

> It has been taught: On that day, Rabbi Eliezer used all the arguments in the world, but they did not accept [them] from him. He said to them: "If the halakhah is in accordance with me, let this carob tree prove [it]." The carob tree was uprooted from its place one hundred cubits—and some say four hundred cubits. They said to him: "One does not bring proof from a carob tree." He said to them: "If the halakhah is in accordance with me, let the channel of water prove [it]." The channel of water turned backward. They said to him: "One does not bring proof from a channel of water." He then said to them: "If the halakhah is in accordance with me, let the walls of the house of study prove [it]." The walls of the house of study leaned to fall. Rabbi Yehoshua rebuked them, [and] said to them: "If talmudic sages argue with one another about the halakhah, what affair is it of yours?" They did not fall, out of respect for Rabbi Yehoshua; but they did not straighten out, out of respect for Rabbi Eliezer, and they still remain leaning. He then said to them: "If the halakhah is in accordance with me, let it be proved from heaven." A

[heavenly] voice went forth and said: "Why are you [disput-
ing] with Rabbi Eliezer, for the halakhah is in accordance
with him everywhere?" Rabbi Yehoshua rose to his feet and
said: "It is not in heaven."

The incredible conclusion of this story is that even when God
Himself intervenes, the sages do not listen: "It is not in heaven."
As in the image of the chain novel, the rabbis understood that it
was their unique role to extend the previous chapters in the best
possible way. A postscript to the story adds that when God saw
Rabbi Yehoshua get up and quote the written Torah against His
own view, "The Holy One, blessed be He . . . smiled and said: `My
sons have defeated Me, My sons have defeated me'" (Bava Metzia
59b). One is cautioned and sobered by the still-leaning walls of the
study house. But ultimately Rabbi Yehoshua's response and dec-
laration are the only correct point of departure for later generations.

The Centrality of Community

The image of participating in writing a chain novel over time
is deeply conservative in a positive sense. Interpreters who seemingly disregard earlier material must show how their alternative
interpretations really fit with the previous chapters. In the absence of strong linkages to the earlier material, novel interpretations lack integrity. Unlike those who walk the paths of discovery
and invention, chain novelists cannot simply push aside inherited
chapters. Accepting the role implies an intense commitment to
the preexisting material. Participants know that what is at stake
is the identity of the community. At any point in its history, the
community is made up of members who actively participate in
the interpretive process. What binds the contemporary community with preceding generations is the method of moral inquiry
even more than the substance. In terms of substance, what is
permitted in one generation is prohibited in the next. What is
constant over time is the self-conscious awareness that the output

of any one generation is part of a much greater whole. The community's project is more than the work of any one generation. Each new generation extends the work of previous generations, and is careful to leave behind a coherent and unified legacy. What is at stake is nothing less than the identity and continuity of the community.

In the following rabbinic midrash (Menahot 29b), Moses is transported through time and finds himself sitting, centuries later, in the academy of Rabbi Akiva. Apparently, Moses cannot understand the complex talmudic discussion there. He becomes perplexed and agitated.

> Rab Judah said in the name of Rab, When Moses ascended on high he found the Holy One, blessed be He, engaged in affixing coronets to the letters. Said Moses, "Lord of the Universe, who stays Thy hand?" He answered, "There will arise a man at the end of many generations, Akiba ben Joseph by name, who will expound upon each tittle heaps and heaps of laws." "Lord of the Universe," said Moses, "permit me to see him." He replied, "Turn thee round." Moses went and sat down behind eight rows [and listened to the discourses upon the law]. Not being able to follow their arguments he was ill at ease, but when they came to a certain subject and the disciples said to the master "Whence do you know it?" and the latter replied, "It is a law given unto Moses at Sinai," he was comforted.

The conclusion of the midrash suggests that Moses is only "comforted" when Rabbi Akiva asserts the connection with Sinai. "It is a law given unto Moses at Sinai" in this instance cannot mean that Moses himself promulgated the specifics of the law. The connection therefore is not a substantive one, but is methodological. Rabbi Akiva is engaged in a process of interpreting the "law given unto Moses at Sinai." Moses is comforted by the knowledge that Rabbi Akiva is extending the written text. Rabbi Akiva's conclusions are not Moses's, but his method is. Moses and Rabbi Akiva are members of the community of Israel by virtue of a common method.

Rabbi Joseph Soloveitchik (1983, p. 120) poetically summarizes and extends the midrash:

> "Moses received the Torah from Sinai, and transmitted it to Joshua," etc. [Avot 1:1]. This is the motto of the *Halakhah.*
> . . . This wondrous chain, which originated on that bright morning of the day of revelation and which stretches forward into eschaton, represents the manner in which the Jewish people experience their own history, a history that floats upon the stormy waters of time. The consciousness of halakhic man, that master of the received tradition, embraces the entire company of the sages of the *masorah* (process of transmission). He lives in their midst, discusses and argues questions of *Halakhah* with them, delves into and analyzes fundamental halakhic principles in their company. All of them merge into one time experience. He walks alongside Maimonides, listens to R. Akiva, senses the presence of Abaye and Raba. He rejoices with them and shares in their sorrow.

The methodology of interpretation is conservative in the very specific sense that it "conserves" the community over time. Interpretation is the identifying mark of membership in the community. Yet, at the very same time that interpretation is conservative, it is also flexible. This point is extremely important for the continued growth and vibrancy of the community. As society changes, its pragmatic needs change. The path of interpretation is well suited to meet the evolving needs of the community. This is especially important for business ethics. As technology develops, as modes of production improve, as organizational structures are refined, as firm size grows, new ethical issues emerge.

The best and most famous example of creative interpretation in the area of business ethics is Hillel's innovation of the *prosbol*. In Deuteronomy 15:1–2 the text reads, "At the end of every seven years thou shalt make a release . . . every creditor shall release that which he hath lent unto his neighbor and his brother; because the Lord's release hath been proclaimed." In the biblical period making loans was viewed as a charitable activity. A debt would only be contracted in case of misery and misfortune. As the economy matured, however, the purpose of lending money changed. Loans were correctly identified as a powerful mechanism for economic development. Those with excess resources could channel their funds into productive activities.

During the first century B.C.E., as commercial life became more complex, Hillel recognized the difficulties of the above legal rule. An inability to collect loans at the end of the seventh year became a hindrance to economic development and communal welfare. The required cancellation of loans after the seventh year created a tremendous barrier to making funds available. Hillel's solution is recorded in the talmudic tractate of Gittin (36a–36b). The *prosbol* is a legal document which allows the lender and borrower to circumvent the cancellation of the debt. According to the Talmud, the text of the *prosbol* read as follows: "I hand over to you, So-and-so, the judges in such-and-such a place, [my bond], so that I may be able to recover any money owing to me from So-and-so at any time I shall desire." The concept underlying the *prosbol* is that while an individual is prohibited from collecting on the loan at the end of the seventh year, the rabbinical court is not. Therefore, the court could collect the funds from the borrower and turn them over to the lender. The effect, of course, was to nullify the law without violating it.

Hillel's *prosbol* was an innovation but not an invention. Importantly, his interpretation was firmly grounded in the biblical text. According to the Sifre, the seemingly superfluous phrase in Deuteronomy 15:3, "but whatsoever of thine is with thy brother thy hand shall release," suggested that contrary to the verse, if the bond was in the hands of the rabbinical court, no release was required. Further, the institution of the *prosbol* can be understood as a fulfillment of Deuteronomy 15:9, where the Bible itself warns:

> Beware that there be not a base thought in thy heart, saying: "The seventh year, the year of release, is at hand," and thine eye be evil against thy needy brother, and thou give him [i.e., lend him] nought; and he cry unto the Eternal One against thee, and it be sin in thee.

This verse might have been read as a warning addressed to the individual, and therefore its fulfillment or nonfulfillment would have been appropriately left to the discretion of each member of the community. However, Hillel creatively chose to read it as an exhortation to the community. The community as a whole has a responsibility to ensure that the needs of the poor are being met. Through the institution of the *prosbol*, Hillel provided a better and more ethically sensitive reading of the biblical material.

Eliezer Berkovits, in his penetrating book, *Not in Heaven: The Nature and Function of Halakha*, catalogues numerous additional instances where Jewish law is interpreted in such a way as to promote economic welfare and thus ensure the continued viability of the community. Pragmatic and moral feasibility are clearly the main considerations of the talmudic regulations in the economic field. They impinge on core institutions. They affect issues of geographic sovereignty, the calendar, employer-employee relationships, and even Temple worship. Among the examples Berkovits lists are the following:

1. During the Second Temple period, rabbinic authorities excluded areas that had previously been part of the Jewish state from the sanctity of Eretz Yisrael. Specifically, the lands of Ammon and Moab, although conquered by Moses and originally included within the boundaries of Israel, were excluded. These lands were thus exempt from the prohibitions of the sabbatical (*sh'mittah*) year. The stated purpose of this ruling was to aid the poor. As the Talmud makes explicit, the "tithe of the poor is to be given in the seventh year" (Y'bamot 16a). Berkovits (1983, p. 14) summarizes further, "the poor would find work in those districts, as well as the other benefits due to them all the time from the yield of the fields."

2. Periodically, the lunar calendar requires an additional thirteenth month. The rabbis ruled that the additional month may never be added during the sabbatical year, when it was prohibited to till the soil (Sanhedrin 12a). The ruling was clearly motivated by reluctance to prolong the prohibition and create additional economic hardships for the people.

3. Generally, in cases of litigation, the imposition of an oath on one of the parties can only free him from payment. As Berkovits explains, "On the strength of an oath one can never gain payment for a claim" (p. 15). The rabbis, however, viewed wage disputes as unique. In the area of employer-employee relations a modification of the general rule was introduced. If the employee claims nonpayment of wages, and the claim is disputed by the employer, the employee takes an oath and is entitled to receive his wages. The talmudic discussion raises an important objection to this ruling. "In what way is the hired laborer different that the rabbis have instituted for him [the privilege] that he should take the oath and receive [his wages]? (Shebu'ot 45a). Two important issues emerge from the ensuing discussion. First, the rabbis, or at least some of the rabbis, deemed the relative wealth of employees and employers as a relevant factor. "Our rabbis removed the oath from the householder and imposed it upon the hired laborer for the sake of his livelihood" (Shebu'ot 54a). Second, the Talmud viewed the employee's statement as less likely to be mistaken. The employer has many employees, but the employee has only one employer.

4. To prevent the exploitation of the poor, the rabbis went so far as to alter certain ritual requirements. For instance, as recounted in Kritut 8a, they changed the law regarding the number of pigeons women had to bring as sacrifices to the Temple after the birth of a child.

> It happened once that the price for two such pigeons went up to a golden dinar. Rabbi Shimon ben Gamliel, the head of the Sanhedrin, then took an oath and said: "I shall not go to bed tonight until the price goes down to a silver dinar." He went into the Beth Hamidrash and taught: "A

woman, even if she gives birth five times, brings only one sacrifice, the rest are no obligation on her." Pretty soon, the price for the pigeons came down to half a dinar.

Rashi, the preeminent talmudic commentator, explains that this case provides an example of changing the law "for the sake of God." There are occasions where the intent of the law requires its alteration and development.

To briefly summarize, these cases demonstrate the flexibility and creativity inherent in the interpretive process. The cases examined are not peripheral issues, but are core concerns of the community. Interpretation at its best is therefore both deeply conservative and flexible enough to ensure the dynamic growth and viability of the community.

The Promise of Transformation

Dworkin (1985, p. 158) wrote, "Now every novelist but the first has the dual responsibilities of interpreting and creating because each must read all that has gone before in order to establish, in the interpretivist sense, what the novel so far created is."

Just as each novelist must determine "what the novel so far created is," so too must each participant in the chain of Jewish tradition determine what the Torah so far created is. The Talmud, for example, declares that the whole of the law is for the purpose of promoting peace (Gittin 59b). If Judaism asks us to transform ourselves both at the level of the individual and at the level of the community, the goal of searching for the meaning (or meanings) inherent in the traditional sources, mitzvot (commandments), customs, and rituals is crucial. If transformation makes sense, one needs to have a vision and purpose in mind. The interpretive process guides, supports, and nurtures the ethical imperative of transformation.

Maimonides is the most well known and eloquent spokesman for the importance of searching out the rational purpose inherent in all mitzvot. In his *Guide for the Perplexed* 3:31, he says:

There is a group of human beings who consider it a grievous thing that causes should be given for any law; what would please them most is that the intellect would not find a meaning for the commandments and prohibitions. What compels them to feel thus is a sickness that they find in their souls, a sickness to which they are unable to give utterance and of which they cannot furnish a satisfactory account. For they think that if those laws were useful in this existence and had been given to us for this or that reason, it would be as if they derived from the reflection and the understanding of some intelligent being. If, however, there is a thing for which the intellect could not find any meaning at all and that does not lead to something useful, it indubitably derives from God; for the reflection of man would not lead to such a thing. . . . It is as if, according to these people of weak intellects, man were more perfect than his Maker; for man speaks and acts in a manner that leads to some intended end, whereas the Deity does not act thus, but commands us to do things that are not useful to us and forbids us to do things that are harmful to us. But He is far exalted above this; the contrary is the case—the whole purpose consisting in what is useful for us.

The contemporary Jewish philosopher David Hartman, in describing the dialectic tension between tradition and change, extends the Maimonidean viewpoint and explores its application to modern economic issues. In an attempt to respect both the classical Jewish tradition and the need for radical transformation, and consistent with Dworkin's metaphor of determining what "the novel so far created is," Hartman (1990, p. 49) writes,

When one enters a totally new frame of reference, no adequate solutions for the development of Halakhah can be found without in some way regaining awareness of the wide range of values that inspired the development of the legal tradition. . . . What we need to learn from the past is not so much how they solved particular problems, or what were the particular forms of their social, economic, and political halakhic frameworks, but rather the underlying spirit and tendency that infused their Halakhah.

Only after uncovering the meaning of the specific halakhic rulings can we legitimately extend and apply the inherited material to modern circumstances.

Hartman (pp. 51–52) boldly applies the method of interpretation to the laws of the sabbatical and Jubilee years.

> We must consider how the concern with egalitarianism, with preventing permanent economic dependence of one social group on another, and with counteracting any sense of total domination over the land or over other human beings, can find expression in contemporary economic and political thought. The biblical warning that exile comes because of the lack of observance of those laws can stimulate us to seek ways of avoiding long-term debts for housing for our children, alienation of workers from creativity, manipulation by concentrations of economic power.
>
> The sabbatical year can have little significance for us if— as happens now—our religious communities are concerned merely with such questions as whether we are permitted to eat the crops of Jewish farmers or only those of non-Jewish ones during that year. We need instead to see the significance of the sabbatical year as an insistence that Sabbath consciousness should not be restricted to notions of intimacy in the life of Jews in their homes, but should also give direction to economic growth in a Jewish society.

Hartman's call for the transformation of the Israeli economy— his specific prescriptions for increasing egalitarianism, counteracting economic exploitation, and enhancing worker creativity— is a legitimate extension of the biblical and rabbinic inheritance. Hartman provides an unusually honest and important example of creative interpretation in the area of Jewish business ethics.

Conclusion

The thesis of this chapter is that Jewish ethics is best thought of as interpretative in character. The path of interpretation is consistent with and promotes the substance of Jewish ethics. Method and substance complement one another. Interpretation is particularly useful for areas of applied ethics, like business.

Unquestionably the method is a risky one. There can be few rules for interpretation. And even if one attempted to construct a set of unchanging and authoritative rules, the rules themselves, if they successfully become part of the tradition, are, in turn, subject to interpretation. Fundamentalist attempts to censor "foreign" or outside values, for example, are doomed to failure. If the so-called foreign values promote a better understanding of who we are and where we should be headed, they are integrated into the tradition, and the newly understood tradition becomes the starting point for the next generation. Interpretation is a method of moral inquiry which provides a tremendous opportunity and demands incredible responsibility. Ultimately, the method is effective only if and when the community takes its mandate seriously.

PART III

EXTENSIONS

He who says "What is mine is mine, and what is yours is yours" is the average type, though some say he is a Sodom-type.

(Ethics of the Fathers 5:13)

The divorce of *Halakha* (Jewish Law) from morality not only eviscerates but falsifies it. (Lichtenstein 1975, p. 106)

6

The Relevance of
"Beyond the Letter of the Law"

The idea of corporate social responsibility is neither new nor radical. The core belief is that business managers, even in their role as business managers, have responsibilities to society beyond profit maximization. Managers, in pursuing their primary goal of increasing shareholder value, have social responsibilities in addition to meeting the minimal requirements of the law. J. Maurice Clark, writing in the *Journal of Political Economy* in 1916, noted that "if men are responsible for the known results of their actions, business responsibilities must include the known results of business dealings, whether or not these have been recognized by law or not" (p. 223).

Nevertheless, the call for increased social responsibility on the part of business managers remains controversial. At least two major perspectives on social responsibility can be isolated. The classical view, most closely identified with Milton Friedman, suggests that social responsibility is incompatible with a free enterprise economy. By contrast, advocates of increased social responsibility point out the desirability of voluntary (and at times costly) corporate activities that promote society's well-being.

The purpose of this chapter is to briefly describe the classical and pro–social responsibility perspectives. We suggest that while important differences in assumptions characterize the two views, there is enough overlap and agreement to move the debate beyond the current stalemate. Specifically, we argue that the concept of *lifnim mishurat hadin*, an innovative and ancient Jewish legal doctrine usually translated as "beyond the letter of the law," might serve as a model for modern legal and social thought. We examine talmudic and post-talmudic sources that apply this concept to the area of business ethics, and explore its applicability to the modern situation. Although the business ethics literature rarely refers to talmudic and rabbinic sources, these texts reflect a sophisticated understanding of business practices and ethical problems.

The most relevant text for our purposes is the following talmudic example (Bava Metzia 83a):

> Some porters [negligently] broke a barrel of wine belonging to Rabbah son of R. Huna. Thereupon Rabbah seized their garments; so the porters went and complained to Rab. "Return the porters their garments," he ordered. "Is that the law?" Rabbah inquired. "Even so," Rab rejoined, "that thou mayest walk in the way of good men." Their garments having been returned, they observed, "We are poor men, have worked all day, and are in need; are we to get nothing?" "Go and pay them," Rab ordered. "Is that the law?" Rabbah asked. "Even so," was Rab's reply, "and keep the path of the righteous."

As the following discussion and analysis of this text makes clear, human beings need unambiguous signals about the contours of proper legal behavior. On the other hand, the inherent limitations of any rule-based legal code present the possibility for unethical and antisocial activities with the law's approval. Jewish law is consciously aware of this tension inherent in all legal codes.

The concept of *lifnim mishurat hadin*, implicitly invoked in the legal case cited above, is offered as a possible solution. Before discussing the case in detail, however, it is useful to briefly survey two alternative contemporary conceptions of business responsibility.

The Classical View

Friedman's position (see Friedman 1962 and 1970; Friedman and Friedman 1980) can be summarized as follows: Business managers have a single responsibility to shareholders, the owners of the corporation: to maximize the firm's value. Managers, acting as agents of the shareholders, have no mandate to embark on projects, however socially responsible, that do not enhance the income-generating ability of the firm. In addition, managers should not refrain from profitable investments that satisfy all legal constraints but do not conform to their own personal social agenda. Rather, as Friedman (1962, p. 133) put it,

> The social responsibility of business is to increase profits.
> . . . Few trends would so thoroughly undermine the very
> foundations of our free society as the acceptance by corpo-
> rate officials of a social responsibility other than to make as
> much money for their stockholders as they possibly can.
> This is a fundamentally subversive doctrine.

Friedman's primary assumption, which leads to his conclusion that social responsibility is a "subversive doctrine," is his belief that the notion of social responsibility as applied to the corporate context, if it means anything at all, implies that the business manager "must act in some way that is not in the interest of his employers" (1970, p. 33). Thus managers who act out of a sense of social responsibility are engaging in a form of taxation without representation.

Further, Friedman believes that business managers have no comparative advantage when it comes to implementing social programs. Managers are experts at producing products, selling them, or financing them. Management does not have the necessary expertise to fight social ills.

We believe that Friedman's argument is both rigorous and somewhat convincing. His voice, although the loudest, clearest, and least apologetic, is by no means solitary. Numerous economists, accountants, sociologists, corporate executives, and social critics, either explicitly or implicitly, accept a similar view of the corporation (Pava and Krausz 1995).

Unquestionably, the most important foundation of the anti-social responsibility view is its insistence that corporate goals must be based on a broad social consensus. According to the classical view, in most, if not all, conceivable cases, the only way for business managers to come to know the social consensus is through the output of the legislature. Rodewald (1987, p. 454) summarized the classical view: "Permit only those deviations from profits that are authorized by law or government regulation so that they will receive the public scrutiny necessary to ensure that they actually reflect widely shared values."

Similarly, David Engel (1979, p. 2), in defending the classical perspective, clarified the starting assumption as follows:

> I will assume that the measures coming out of the legislative process either accurately reflect the political will of the relevant constituencies—on the basis of facts known—or may be taken to reflect that will because of a widely shared acceptance of legitimacy. What is perhaps more extreme, I will assume that, at least in the long run, even legislative inaction should be taken to reflect political consensus—a consensus that nothing should be done about a particular matter.

Anyone calling for increased social responsibility on the part of management must be able to answer the question "why any given goal, if in fact the object of a social consensus, has not been placed or given sufficient weight by the legislature in the profit-maximization proxy" (ibid., p. 36).

We close this brief summary of the classical view by para-phrasing its most powerful insight. If a democratic society wants businesses to engage in, or refrain from, specific activities, it can always enact laws to control corporate behavior. The absence of specific legislation implies the existence of a consensus that nothing should be done.

Social Responsibility Advocates

Consider the following cases, all of which have occurred within the last year or so.

1. According to the *New York Times*, a gun producer intends to begin manufacturing a new bullet which, after entering the body, explodes inside the victim, making it almost impossible for a doctor to surgically remove it.

2. A record company faced intense public pressure over its release of a record album advocating the killing of police officers.

3. A beer distillery was severely criticized for specifically marketing a high-alcohol malt liquor in poor urban areas.

4. A newspaper refused a request to refrain from printing advertisements by the Kingdom of Saudi Arabia (which is openly antisemitic and sexist in its employment practices), arguing that it would not pursue its editorial policy through the acceptance or nonacceptance of advertising.

Question: Can and should managers in these corporations explore the ethical and moral responsibilities of their business decisions? Does there exist a class of cases where managers should forgo profits in order to pursue perceived social responsibilities? Advocates of increased corporate social responsibility believe that the answers to these questions are obvious. Even if management is convinced that long-run profits might be enhanced by the production of a technologically sophisticated and deadly bullet, they have a right, and even an obligation, to say no. Managers of record companies and beer distilleries must pursue both the financial and the ethical implications of marketing their products. It is justifiable for a newspaper, especially a newspaper which advocates increased corporate social responsibility for other businesses, to pursue its editorial policy through its own business practices. In each of these four cases, the answer is that business managers must consider their ethical and moral responsibilities.

Clarence C. Walton, in *The Moral Manager* (1988), describes the organizational philosophy underlying the pro–social responsibility movement as "covenant ethics," as opposed to "contract ethics." Walton notes (p. 209), "The covenant model . . . draws much of its inspiration from religion and places people above pockets: to belong to a community is to have claims upon it." He goes on to argue (p. 210) that the advantage of the covenant model "is that it invites leaders to take a large view of their responsibilities because, under it, corporations are seen as much as moral organizations as they are money-making machines."

Advocates of increased social responsibility point out the limitations inherent in a complete reliance on the law. Christopher D. Stone, in *Where the Law Ends: The Social Control of Corporate Behavior* (1975), provides the most exhaustive discussion of this topic. He describes general reasons why the law is limited in terms of what it can accomplish. Among his reasons are the time-lag problem and the limitations connected with making and implementing the law.

The time-lag problem suggests that the law is "primarily a reactive institution" (p. 94). Therefore there may be a significant interval between the time when a problem is recognized and the legislature's passing of a law to solve it. Until new laws are passed, "a great deal of damage—some irreversible—can be done" (p. 94). Socially responsible managers, therefore, should not exploit a situation by quickly engaging in an activity when the legislature simply has not had time to act.

One of the most important problems associated with the limitations connected with making laws is the significant information gap between legislators and corporate managers. Stone (p. 96) makes the point as follows:

> But when we attempt to legislate in more complex areas, we find an information gap. Even the specialized regulatory

agencies, much less the Congress, cannot in their rule-making capacities keep technically abreast of the industry. Are employees who work around asbestos being subjected to high risks of cancer? What psychological and physical dangers lurk in various forms of manufacturing processes? . . . Congress and the various regulatory bodies can barely begin to answer these questions. The companies most closely associated with the problems may not know the answers either; but they certainly have the more ready access to the most probative information.

Again, it is unthinkable for corporate managers to engage in activities which the legislature would undoubtedly prohibit if it possessed the same information as management.

Stone, in line with other pro–social responsibility advocates, concludes his survey as follows (p. 110):

If the agencies—or the other public control mechanisms— were effective, then it would be proper to brush aside the calls for corporate social responsibility by calling on the law to keep corporations in line. But the weaknesses of the agencies are simply a further argument that trust in our traditional legal machinery as a means of keeping corporations in bounds is misplaced—and that therefore something more is needed.

That "something more" is, of course, increased social responsibility on the part of corporations.

Areas of Agreement

Undoubtedly a wide chasm separates the classical view from the pro–social responsibility perspective. Nevertheless, the differences should not be overstated.

For example, having spelled out above what we believe is an unbiased view of Friedman's writings, it should be pointed out that even his "unequivocal" argument against social responsibility is ambiguous enough to provide some sanction for corporate managers to engage in what they might view as socially responsible actions. In describing the proper role for corporate executives, Friedman (1970, p. 33) has written that their responsibility is to conduct the business in accordance with the desires of stockholders, "which generally will be to make as much money as possible *while conforming to the basic rules of the society, both those embodied in law and those embodied in ethical custom*" (emphasis added).

Although he certainly does not accept the term "social responsibility," even Friedman recognizes the existence of corporate obligations beyond mere legal requirements. Even corporate managers of the Friedman type need to make moral decisions about "ethical custom," and cannot escape formulating an answer to Friedman's rhetorical question (1962, p. 133): "If businessmen do have social responsibility other than maximizing profits for stockholders, how are they to know what it is?" The onus is on the defenders of the classical view to spell out precisely how this question is different in kind from the following: If businessmen need to conform to the basic rules of society, which include what is embodied in "ethical custom," how are they to know what the rules are?

Similarly, pro–social responsibility advocates recognize the truth and advantages inherent in their opponents' view. Even while advocating the covenant approach, Clarence Walton (1983, p. 209) clearly describes the benefits of a classical "contractual" approach.

> To define the covenant model as humanitarian and the contract model as narrowly economic is misplaced. Contractualists are also interested in humans. What they say is that the fruits of organized efforts should be allocated strictly on the basis of contributions and since one normally cannot hire workers without first securing capital, providers of capital come first. Furthermore, in today's world and particularly in large organizations, principals often come

out a poor second. Agents can and do negotiate deals with substantial, if not total, indifference toward the principals: doctors use hospitals for their own practices; professors exploit institutional prestige to secure lucrative consulting assignments; and managers run fantastic aerial displays with golden parachutes. When concern for principals is minimized, injustices occur.

Further, we believe that with regard to at least three extremely important areas of business conduct, consensus between the classical and pro–social responsibility views is likely to emerge: obedience to the law, corporate disclosure, and reducing political activity on the part of corporations.

Even if we are correct and a limited consensus is emerging, a complete synthesis—a perspective that would meet the non-negotiable demands of both classical and pro–social responsibility advocates—eludes us. However, we believe that talmudic law, and in particular the legal concept of *lifnim mishurat hadin* ("beyond the letter of the law") represents a viable legal mechanism to push the debate beyond its current stalemate.

Talmudic Law and Business Responsibility

Nahmanides (Spain, 1194–1270), one of the greatest Jewish scholars of the Middle Ages, described the individual who exploited the limitations of the law as a "scoundrel within the law." The talmudic solution to this problem, as illustrated in the case quoted above, is the meta-legal mechanism known as *lifnim mishurat hadin*.

Recall the facts of the case: Rabbah hired porters to transport a barrel of wine. In carrying out the assigned task, the porters negligently broke the barrel, and therefore Rabbah's wine was lost. Reading between the lines and teasing out the text (an indispensable task when interpreting a talmudic case), the porters apparently took Rabbah to a local court and "sued" for the return of their garments and payment of their daily wages. Rab, acting as the judge or arbitrator, knows of no specific legal ruling that controls the case and obligates Rabbah to return the garments in question. Certainly, there is no explicit obligation recorded in any legal code requiring payment of the wages. However, Rab determined that "even so" Rabbah should (according to some interpretations, must) return the garments and pay the employees their wages. The scriptural evidence quoted by Rab suggests that the concept of *lifnim mishurat hadin* is at work here.

Nahmanides, commenting on the general command in Deuteronomy (6:18) to pursue "the right and the good," further elaborated on *lifnim mishurat hadin* (quoted in Lichtenstein 1978, p. 108).

> For it is impossible to mention in the Torah all of a person's actions toward his neighbors and acquaintances, all of his commercial activity, and all social and political institutions. So after He had mentioned many of them such as, "Thou shalt not go about as a tale-bearer," "Thou shalt not stand by idly by the blood of thy fellow," "Thou shalt not curse the deaf," "Thou shalt rise up before age," and the like, the Torah resumes to say generally that one should do the good and the right in all matters, to the point that there are included in this compromise, *lifnim mishurat hadin* . . .

In the talmudic case in question, Rab determined that although no specific legal rule explicitly stated Rabbah's obligations to his employees, the general biblical obligation to "pursue the right and the good" demanded that the employer compensate his employees.

The modern talmudic translator and scholar Adin Steinsaltz (1990) further explains *lifnim mishurat hadin* in his discussion at Bava Metzia 30b.

> Beyond the letter of the law implies the exercise of restraint in claiming one's due, so as to fulfill a religious commandment. In the context of a person's duty to God, such conduct is generally called "the beautification of a

commandment"—and usually involves carrying it out with extra scrupulousness. But in commercial relationships the expression . . . is used to describe a situation where one person does a favor for another although he is not strictly obliged to do so by the Halakhah (Jewish Law). Generally the Sages are of the opinion that, the greater a person is, the more he is morally obliged to behave "beyond the requirements of the law" and to exact less than the full right to which he is legally entitled."

In "Does Jewish Tradition Recognize an Ethic Independent of Halakha?" (1978), Aharon Lichtenstein clarifies the parameters of this issue. Because of the great importance of his essay for our present purposes, we will examine it extensively.

Lichtenstein's View of *Lifnim Mishurat Hadin*

Lichtenstein begins by noting that "if we equate Halakha with the *din* (specific legal rulings); if we mean that everything can be looked up, every moral dilemma resolved by reference to code or canon, the notion is both palpably naive and patently false. . . . There are moments when one must seek independent counsels" (p. 107) In other words, Lichtenstein is suggesting, even in a system of law which believers claim has divine sanction, a system of law which is unparalleled in terms of its detailed legislation, one can in no way neatly disentangle legal obligations from moral responsibilities. "The divorce of Halakha from morality not only eviscerates but falsifies it" (p. 106).

Lichtenstein disagrees with Steinsaltz's characterization of *lifnim mishurat hadin* as constituting a "favor." Rather, and this is his most important observation, the "thoroughly mandatory elements" of *lifnim mishurat hadin* clearly indicate that "it is no mere option" (p. 109). According to Lichtenstein, "the Halakha is multiplanar and many-dimensional; that, properly conceived, it includes much more than is explicitly required or permitted by specific rules, we shall realize that the ethical moment we are seeking is itself an aspect of Halakha. The demand or, if you will, the impetus for transcending the *din* is itself part of the halakhic corpus" (p. 109).

According to this view, the gulf that separates law and morality is made smaller by the law's formally incorporating ethical language and explicitly recognizing its own inherent limitations. The talmudic view suggests that the law can successfully carve out a domain in which individuals are expected and encouraged to apply ethical and extralegal criteria. The concept of *lifnim mishurat hadin,* as understood by Lichtenstein, meets the most important demand of the classical view, articulated above, head-on. The classical view demands that managers "should pursue only those social goals clearly signalled to them as supported by a social consensus" (Engel 1979, p. 35). While the legislature cannot always enact explicit rules demanding or prohibiting particular goals and behavior, it can do the next best thing. A system of law, talmudic law included, can carefully and self-consciously state its belief that there exists a class of cases in which individuals are expected to behave in an ethical fashion. By incorporating a concept like *lifnim mishurat hadin,* a legislature can clearly signal society's expectation that businesses, like individuals, accept social responsibilities beyond profit maximization. There is a sphere of activity in which contextual morality predominates. As an aside, it would appear that the proliferation of corporate codes of conduct reflects the recognition by individual corporations of employee obligations beyond legal requirements. For example, Stevens (1994, p. 64) noted that codes are managerial tools for shaping change. "They often demand from employees higher standards of behavior than required by law."

Lichtenstein's discussion of the need for and benefits of *lifnim mishurat hadin* in talmudic law provides interesting and important insights useful to understanding the current debate between the classical and pro–social responsibility views.

As in the classical view, Lichtenstein notes that the more carefully a legal code describes its rules, and the more systematically and rigorously it specifies novel cases and applications, the better the legal code. He writes as follows (p. 115):

The formalist is guided by a principle or a rule governing a category of cases defined by n number of characteristics. The more sensitive and sophisticated the system, the more individuated the categories. Whatever the degree of specificity, however, the modus operandi is the same: action grows out of the application of class rules to a particular case judged to be an instance of that class or of the interaction of several classes, there being, of course principles to govern seemingly hybrid cases as well.

In this paragraph Lichtenstein describes what we consider the paradigmatic contractual approach, to borrow Walton's phrase. The code of law anticipates particular classes of cases and develops directives to be followed. It sets up general rules which are then applied on a case-by-case basis. Individual cases share enough similar characteristics to make this approach viable. Lichtenstein further amplifies that judgments are essentially grounded in deductive reasoning. "Metaphors that speak of laws as controlling or governing a case are therefore perfectly accurate" (p. 115).

Jewish law, as discussed in the talmudic sources, is contractual. Nevertheless, describing it as wholly contractual is incorrect. Integrated as an essential component of Jewish law is the notion that a code-based system of laws (while necessary) is in no way sufficient. The meta-halakhic concept of *lifnim mishurat hadin* explicitly recognizes the inherent limitations of any conceivable code of laws, even in the case of halakhah, a code presumed to be of divine origin. Therefore Jewish law can be described as incorporating the covenantal approach as a meta-concept, above and beyond the contractual approach. According to the Talmud, business contracts and laws presuppose the existence of an overarching covenantal worldview.[1]

Lifnim Mishurat Hadin and the Modern Situation

The underlying strength of the pro–social responsibility perspective is its insistence on recognizing felt moral obligations

beyond legal requirements. Lichtenstein's existential pronounce-
ment about the limitations of the halakhah would seem to apply
even more directly to American law: "Which of us has not, at
times, been made painfully aware of the ethical paucity of his
legal resources who has not found that the fulfillment of explicit
halakhic duty could fall well short of exhausting clearly felt moral
responsibility?" (p. 107). *Lifnim mishurat hadin,* by explicitly allowing and encouraging ethical behavior in certain prescribed areas,
helps "fill a moral lacuna" (ibid.).

The law, by carving out a domain in which individuals are
expected to apply ethical criteria, recognizes and benefits from
the advantages of contextual morality. Contextual morality is
more flexible, its duty more readily definable in light of the
specific characteristics of unique situations, as Lichtenstein (p.
115) explains in the following passage:

> The contextualist ... will have nothing to do with middle-
> distance guidelines. He is directed, in theory, at least, only
> by the most universal and the most local of factors—by a
> minimal number, perhaps as few as one or two, of ultimate
> values, on the one hand, and by the unique contours of the
> situation at hand, on the other. Guided by his polestar(s), the
> contextualist employs his moral sense (to use an outdated
> but still useful eighteenth-century term) to evaluate and
> intuit the best way of eliciting maximal good from the exis-
> tential predicament confronting him. A nominalist in ethics,
> he does not merely contend that every case is phenomeno-
> logically different. That would be a virtual truism. He ar-
> gues that the differences are generally so crucial that no
> meaningful directives can be formulated.

The late Thomas "Tip" O'Neill, former Speaker of the U.S.
House of Representatives, was fond of saying that all politics is
local. It is equally true that all ethics is local. The concept of *lifnim
mishurat hadin* allows decision makers the flexibility of incorporating local knowledge. Thus the important "information gap"
between business decision makers and legislators can be circum-

vented. As Lichtenstein further points out, the demands of *lifnim mishurat hadin* evolve from a specific situation.

The formal integration of *lifnim mishurat hadin* within the legal system provides guidance (although not direct answers) for decisions falling outside specific legal rules. One looks back, as it were, to the legal code, to formulate an answer to the following question: Given the current legal code, what would the law have decided, had it known everything that I now know? Lichtenstein (p. 117) notes that by applying the law "to circumstances beyond its legal pale but nevertheless sufficiently similar to share a specific telos," the scope of the law is enlarged.

A major advantage of *lifnim mishurat hadin* is its dependence on the individual. In those areas in which *lifnim mishurat hadin* is operative, individual choice is called for. "Only direct ad hoc judgment, usually—although this is logically a wholly separate question—his own, can serve as an operative basis for decision. Between ultimate value and immediate issue, there can be no other midwife" (pp. 115–116). Many of the core issues that constitute the social responsibility agenda are best dealt with by private individuals rather than the state. For example, issues like increasing employee autonomy, equal pay for equal work, affirmative action, philanthropic activities, and meeting the needs of local communities are best dealt with by those who are involved in the day-to-day business activities, i.e., the business managers. Decision making in these areas requires intimate knowledge of institutional detail. Here we should not overstate the case. Some issues, like environmental pollution and investment in foreign countries, are better left to a legislature. Our point is merely that some issues are appropriately assigned to individual businesses to formulate the "correct" ethical responses and to draw the precise contours of perceived social responsibility.

Jewish law provides an example of a legal system which has successfully integrated the most important concerns of both the classical and the pro–social responsibility perspectives. On the one hand, by explicitly incorporating the concept of *lifnim mishurat hadin* into the legal system, pro–social responsibility advocates have an answer to the question of why the legislature might not have acted in a particular case. The legislature itself formally recognizes its own inherent limitations. On the other hand, business managers need not ignore their "moral sense" and dismiss the possibility of engaging in socially responsible activities. No code of laws can articulate a set of rules that would exhaust ethical responsibilities.

Undoubtedly, the success of the Jewish legal system in general, and its ability to integrate the concept of *lifnim mishurat hadin* in particular, is inextricably linked to the particular situation in which talmudic law evolved. This situation was characterized by (1) a homogeneous culture, (2) a shared belief in the divine authorship of the legal system, (3) a universally accepted concept of covenant, (4) a preindustrial society, (5) small-scale business, and (6) primitive technology. The legal system could assume, at least to a first approximation, the existence of a shared sense of ethics. Participants in the economy had a deep and sure sense of their social responsibilities and obligations. The small scale of business, the slow pace of change, similar educational backgrounds, the realization that business exchanges were conducted within a strong communal network are all powerful reasons to expect a reasonably effective integration of law and ethics.

Nevertheless, as the case we are analyzing suggests, differences of opinion could emerge. "Even so," even in situations of dispute, we saw that the judge could rule that Rabbah must return the garments in question and pay the porters their wages.

As traditional modes of living give way to modern, complex, multicultural societies, where business is conducted on a huge and unprecedented level, we need to be careful about importing traditional solutions. Severing the concept of *lifnim mishurat hadin* from the rest of the corpus of Jewish law and culture and adapting it to contemporary conditions is like a doctor removing a heart from one living species and transplanting it to another. The transplant must be carefully planned out, and differences between the two species must be thoughtfully documented.

On the other hand, the rapid changes in society underscore the impossibility of relying completely on a law-based system. The Jewish perspective on this point is remarkably similar to

Michael Novak's description of the Catholic approach. The church, according to Novak (1993), can affirm capitalism under two restrictive conditions. First, legitimate capitalism must be constrained by a "strong judicial framework which places it at the service of human freedom in its totality" (p. 977). Second, capitalism must be balanced by "a set of moral-cultural institutions that embody the Western religious and philosophical tradition of virtue" (p. 977). In other words, capitalism needs to integrate both law and ethics. The concept of *lifnim mishurat hadin* attempts at this integration.

We conclude this chapter by noting the extreme importance that the Talmud attributed to the concept of *lifnim mishurat hadin*. In trying to understand the reasons why Jerusalem and the Temple were destroyed, the rabbis (Bava Metzia 30b) declared:

> For R. Yohanan said: Jerusalem was destroyed only because they gave judgments therein in accordance with biblical law. Were they then to have judged in accordance with untrained arbitrators? But say thus: because they based their judgments [strictly] upon biblical law, and did not go beyond the letter of the law (*lifnim mishurat hadin*).

Lifnim mishurat hadin is thought to be the glue that held the commonwealth together. It is an idea that resonates beyond talmudic law.

---

[1] (See Page 153) The argument put forth here is not meant to suggest that Jewish law condones all social-responsibility activities. For example, Aaron Levine (1994) has suggested that, at least in the area of corporate philanthropy, Jewish law might actually prohibit managers from donating corporate funds to charity. Citing evidence from Rabbi Moses Isserles, Levine writes that "even when a business entity operates under an implicit mandate to devote a specific percentage of its profits to charity, the disposition of the charity funds is a matter of individual shareholder prerogative and does not fall under the purview of the business entity. How much more so does this judgment hold when the business entity operates without any understanding that a portion of its profits shall be devoted to charity" (p. 15).

7

Joseph and the Use of Inside Information

This chapter differs from most of the rest of the book in two ways. First, the presentation here underscores the importance of utilizing narrative material as well as legal texts. Religious narrative provides an additional dimension by which to understand Jewish business ethics. The many biblical and rabbinic stories provide important insights that are not available from a purely legalistic approach to business ethics. The narrative material often offers a greater depth and texture to the business ethics discussion. In addition, this chapter focuses, to a large extent, on economy-wide concerns, as opposed to individual and organizational ethics.

According to midrashic literature, Joseph, alone among our forefathers, is considered a *zaddik* (righteous person). In *Messengers of God,* Elie Wiesel (1976) asks why our rabbis described him in such lofty terms. After all, the Torah explicitly writes that Joseph brings to his father an "evil report" about his brothers (see Genesis 37:2). Furthermore, Joseph marries the daughter of an Egyptian priest, raises his children among pagans, and, seemingly, leads a life of luxury among the Egyptian elite. In what sense then is Joseph a *zaddik*? To resolve the contradiction Wiesel (p. 168) writes: "There is in Joseph a duality which influences his deeds and his choices and makes him into a genuine, therefore torn person. He lived on two levels, in two worlds, tossed back and forth by frequently contradictory forces."

Part of Wiesel's answer is that Joseph is able to bridge two distinct worlds. He lives both in the world of his fathers and in the world of the Egyptians. His "exile" is very different from that of Jacob, his father. Jacob lives with Laban, but is able to summarize his life there with the terse phrase, "I have sojourned with Laban" (Genesis 32:4). As Rashi explains, "I have become neither a prince nor other person of importance, but merely a sojourner." This is in stark contrast to Joseph, who participates in and contributes to his political and cultural surroundings. In contrast to Jacob, he is not merely a sojourner, but, in fact, rises to the highest rank in Egyptian society. Joseph's life can be characterized as one of positive synthesis. He functions simultaneously in two worlds. It is precisely because of his attainments in Egypt that Joseph is able to save his family from hunger.

The purpose of this chapter is to examine and understand two important events in Joseph's life in light of recent economic theory. By focusing on the economic concept of inside information and on other economic insights, a new, albeit experimental view of the Joseph narrative emerges.

Inside Information: Morally Neutral

I focus on two episodes in Joseph's career in which he possesses inside information. Before considering these two episodes, however, it is helpful to define and clarify this term. Inside information, as an economic concept, grew out of the innovative, but simple, idea that information—like physical assets—is a scarce economic resource. In classical economic theory, all participants in the economy, consumers as well as producers, were assumed to be endowed with sufficient information to rationally allocate resources in the most efficient manner. More recent theories, however, have suggested that powerful insights about human behavior can be generated by using more realistic details in describing the economy. Indeed, economists have suggested that in reality information is spotty, biased, and very costly to obtain (Akerlof 1970). For example, it is often a time-consuming and difficult chore to determine which vendor is selling a product at the lowest price, or which firm is offering the highest salaries to prospective employees. In this context, an individual in possession of information that is not freely available may control a valuable asset.

We define inside information in very general terms as "information asymmetry." One party to a transaction possesses certain information, while a second party to the same transaction does not. Under this definition, possessing inside information is not unethical. Rather, it is merely a descriptive term which carries no ethical implications. It is morally neutral.

The notion of inside information is usually applied by economists to business corporations. The managers of a corporation are assumed to be in possession of (inside) information to which the outside shareholders do not have access. Simply by virtue of the fact that they are making business decisions on a day-to-day basis, coupled with their access to the corporation's internal records, managers have an informational advantage over shareholders. A much-discussed example of inside information in a business setting is foreknowledge of a pending corporate takeover. Given that stock market prices generally soar after the public announcement of a takeover, this information is extremely valuable. A typical economic study will examine the kinds of contracts and agreements that emerge out of situations characterized by inside information. A recent study, for example, concluded that one of the functions of financial accounting is to mitigate the problems associated with inside information (Watts and Zimmerman 1986). In the broadest strokes, one can summarize this research as that area of economics which explains how human relationships are affected by information asymmetries.

Joseph's Inside Information

In what sense does Joseph possess inside information? How does he use his inside information? And, finally, how are human relationships affected by the information asymmetries? The two cases that we will examine are (1) Joseph's prophecy (prediction) of seven good years followed by seven bad years, and (2) his informational advantage over his brothers concerning his identity.

Both of these cases satisfy our definition of inside information. Joseph has perfect information regarding future economic conditions in Egypt. It is inside information to the extent that the inhabitants of Egypt do not have access to this knowledge. His informational advantage over his brothers concerning his identity is also a case of inside information in the general sense that we defined it above. Joseph has information about his own identity, and his brothers do not. The text in Genesis clearly indicates the advantage that Joseph enjoys over his brothers. That our second case does not deal with pecuniary matters does not affect its classification as a case of inside information. Inside information is a general concept that is useful in a variety of contexts. The selection and discussion of this second case also serves to underscore that the possession of inside information is morally neutral.

Pharaoh's Dream

First, we will examine Joseph's prophecy of seven good years followed by seven bad years. The details of how he comes into possession of his inside information are familiar. The Torah is explicit on this point. "Not I, God will answer the peace of Pharaoh" (Genesis 41:16). Although some may consider Joseph to have been the first economist, that is not the position adopted here. Joseph does not make an economic forecast based on scientific methodology, but rather is interpreting a dream. His methodology is not economics, but a form of prophecy. One difference is that, while prophecy provides perfect information, economic forecasting is less than perfect. Economic forecasting is based on historical relationships, and assumes that past relationships among economic variables will persist into the future.

While there is consensus among commentators as to the source of Joseph's prediction, there is no agreement as to the source of

Joseph's policy prescription. Following the interpretation of Pharaoh's dreams, Joseph adds the following (Genesis 41:33–36):

> Now therefore let Pharaoh look out a man understanding and wise, and set him over the land of Egypt. Let Pharaoh do this, and let him appoint overseers over the land, and take up the fifth part of the land of Egypt in the seven years of plenty. And let them store up all the food of those good years that come, and pile up corn under the hand of Pharaoh, for food in the cities and let them keep it. And the food shall be as a charge for the land against the seven years of famine, which shall be in the land of Egypt; that the land be not cut off through the famine.

There are (at least) two views concerning the policy prescription described in the preceding verses. The first view, that of Ramban (Nahmanides) and others, states that the prescription is essentially part of the interpretation. The second view, that of Rashi, argues that while the prediction itself is from God, the policy prescription is not.

Nehama Leibowitz (1981, p. 444) writes that "The difference between Rashi and Ramban lies chiefly in their understanding of the metaphorical implication of the term `eating up' or `devouring'." According to Ramban, "Had they commissioned him to advise the king? It was merely part-and-parcel of the dream's interpretation." Ramban argues that the lean cows "eating up" the fat cows symbolized the policy prescription. The dream indicates that survival in the famine years would be possible only by storing the food during the years of plenty. Ramban continues, "This is not according to Rashi, who states that `all the plenty shall be forgotten' is the interpretation of the `eating up'."

Further, Leibowitz makes the point that, even according to Ramban, "there is no correspondence between the details of Joseph's plan and the dream." Therefore, we can summarize by stating that while there is some disagreement between Rashi and Ramban, both agree that the details of Joseph's interpretation are of his own invention. In fact, Ramban writes, "Joseph said all of this so that he [Pharaoh] would select him; for the eyes of the wise man are in his head," a seeming criticism of Joseph's advice.

Centralization and Inside Information

It is helpful at this point to more fully examine the details of Joseph's policy prescription, keeping in mind both his informational advantage and the fact that he is the originator of the plan.

Certainly the main characteristic of the plan is its emphasis on central planning. "Let Pharaoh do this . . . and pile up corn *under the hand of Pharaoh*, for food in the cities, and let them keep it" (Genesis 41:34–35, emphasis added). Pharaoh is in control of food collection and food distribution. Leibowitz (1981, p. 525) writes,

> We have here the first example of land nationalization or, as a contemporary writer expresses it, control, centralization of food supply, and equal distribution accompanied by the nationalization of private property, first of money, then cattle, and finally, land. Henceforth all the lessees of Pharaoh's land pay him "the state" ground rent and live on the residue.

Along with central planning, a second characteristic of Joseph's plan, left out of Leibowitz's analysis, revolves around his use of inside information.

Why does Joseph keep the information private? In economic terms, why does Joseph abandon the concept of full disclosure? An alternative solution clearly could have been to publicize his forecast and allow the market to solve the problem. Given the information that the seven good years would be followed by seven bad years, a free market could adjust, and, arguably, allocate food more efficiently than Joseph's central-planning solution. Thousands of individual producers would have competed amongst themselves to satisfy the future needs of the inhabitants. Even if Joseph believed that there was a role for a central government to play, he might still have publicized the information and adopted a mixed-economy solution. This alternative would have allowed the government to gather the food, but would have also allowed individuals to make their own arrangements. In a mixed economy, neither the government nor private individuals monopolize trade.

Even more importantly, perhaps, a solution that emphasized the free market would have prevented Pharaoh from obtaining the inordinate power and wealth that he eventually amassed. Recent empirical evidence from Eastern Europe and the Soviet Union underscores these points and has convinced even the most orthodox of socialists of the benefits of a free economy. One of the least understood aspects of a free economy is the benefits derived from sharing information among economic agents. Indeed, if one were to evaluate Joseph's plan in purely economic terms, it would be considered a failure. There is a hint of this in the verse "And the thing was good in the eyes of Pharaoh, and in the eyes of all his servants" (Genesis 41:37). By explicitly stating that the plan was perceived as positive from Pharaoh's perspective, the verse may be interpreted as an ironic comment suggesting that it was *only* positive from his perspective. Generally, what is good for the leaders, particularly a leader like Pharaoh, is not good for society at large.

Theoretically, it has been argued that economic freedom is inextricably interwoven with political freedom. Joseph's abandonment of economic freedom, through concealing his inside information and through his detailed program for setting up a state-controlled economy, inevitably leads to political slavery. It is important to note that we are in no way assigning blame to Joseph. The Genesis text is clear that it was God's plan, from the outset, that Abraham's descendants would be enslaved in Egypt. The biblical assumption is that God works through various human messengers and agents to bring about His desired results. In this case, Joseph was simply carrying out the divine plan, albeit unwittingly. In fact Joseph's words to his brothers concerning their "blame" in selling him into slavery apply all the more to Joseph himself. After revealing himself to his brothers, he eloquently reminds them as follows: "Now therefore be not grieved, nor angry with yourselves, that ye sold me hither: for God did send me before you for the preservation of life" (Genesis 45:6).

On the relationship between economics and politics, Milton Friedman (1962, p. 8) writes:

> Economic arrangements play a dual role in the promotion of a free society. On the one hand, freedom in economic arrangements is itself a component of freedom broadly understood, so economic freedom is an end in itself. In the second place, economic freedom is also an indispensable means toward the achievement of political freedom.

This narrative provides the classic example of what F. A. Hayek called the "road to serfdom." In his famous book by this title, Hayek showed how economic freedom is linked to political freedom, and argued that without economic freedom, society is doomed to political slavery as well. Hayek (1944, p. 91) put it as follows: "Economic planning would not affect merely those of our marginal needs that we have in mind when we speak contemptuously about the merely economic. It would, in effect, mean that we as individuals should no longer be allowed to decide what we regard as marginal." As a direct result of Joseph's policy, Egypt becomes a slave state. In a culture which accepts slavery, Pharaoh's ultimate plan to enslave the Jewish people is widely accepted. Once one accepts the idea of slavery for one group of people, it is easier to accept it for another group, especially a group of foreign Hebrews.

Once again we emphasize that the issue established here is that Joseph made an economic blunder, not a spiritual or moral error. In fact, the analysis here is not intended as criticism of Joseph. Given his economic knowledge, his solution may have been the best possible one, and in this sense would not even be considered an economic blunder. It is in the context of modern economic theory, recent empirical evidence, and our reading of the relevant biblical verses that the judgment is made.

A close reading of the relevant verses (Genesis 41:53–56) bears out this interpretation.

> And the seven years of plenty, that was in the land of Egypt, were finished. And the seven years of famine began to come, according as Joseph had said: and the famine was in all lands; but in the land of Egypt there was bread. And when all the land of Egypt was famished, the *people cried to Pharaoh for bread* [emphasis added]; and Pharaoh said unto all Egypt, "Go unto Joseph; what he saith to you, do." And the famine was over all the face of the earth: and Joseph opened all the places that had food in them and sold grain unto the Egyptians; and the famine waxed sore in the land of Egypt.

The people had been denied the inside information. They had no idea that the seven good years would be followed by the seven bad years. Had Joseph publicized this information, would the people have been put into the position where they had cry to Pharaoh for bread? Even at this early stage of the famine, one gets a clear sense of the new dependency the people have toward Pharaoh. The *Or ha-Hayyim* commentary, discussing why Joseph needed to open *all* the storage areas at this early stage, says (as summarized in Leibowitz 1982): "Since one who has bread in his basket cannot be compared to one who has not [*sic*]. He therefore meant to satisfy the psychological feeling of want by opening the granaries for them to see the plenty garnered there and rest secure."

The *Or ha-Hayyim* seems to imply that the people's need to see all the stored food is based merely on a psychological need. The position adopted here is that this cry represents the first realization by the people of their utter dependency. Perhaps Joseph is forced to open the granaries, not for a psychological need, but to signal his benevolent intentions.

As the famine intensified, the dependency became more encompassing. We read (Genesis 47:13–17):

> And there was no bread in all the land; for the famine was very heavy, so that the land of Egypt and all the land of Canaan fainted by reason of the famine. And Joseph collected all the money that was found in the land of Egypt, and in the land of Canaan, for the corn which they bought: and Joseph brought the money into Pharaoh's house. And when the money was exhausted in the land of Egypt, and in the land of Canaan, all the Egyptians came unto Joseph, and said "Give us bread: for why should we die in thy presence? for the money is at an end." And Joseph said, "Come, give your cattle; and I will give you for your cattle, if money is at an end." And they brought their cattle unto Joseph: and Joseph gave them bread in exchange for horses, and for the flocks, and for the cattle of the herds, and for the asses: and he fed them with bread for all their cattle for that year.

At this second stage, Joseph gains control of both the monetary assets (money) and the capital assets of an agricultural society (cattle, horses, flocks, and asses). Given the state monopoly, Joseph is able to draw up the terms of the exchange, any terms he wants.

As time passes, the famine continues to intensify. The Torah (Genesis 47:18–19) relates:

> When that year was ended, they came unto him the second year, and said unto him, "We will not withhold from my lord, that our money is exhausted; my lord also hath our herds of cattle: nothing remains before my lord, but our bodies, and our ground: Wherefore shall we die before thine eyes, both we and our ground? buy us and our ground for bread, and we and our ground will be *servants unto Pharaoh* [emphasis added] and give us seed, that we may live, and not die, that the ground be not desolate."

At this final stage, the people are literally willing to give up everything, including mastery over their own bodies, in order to survive. A key word in these verses is "servants." The dependency is now complete. The people are willing to sell themselves as slaves (servants) unto Pharaoh. While it is debatable whether or not Joseph took them up on the offer, the willingness to sell themselves into slavery and the ensuing loss of dignity is not. Ramban, for example, argues that Joseph did not enslave the people. For evidence that Joseph actually did enslave the people, see Genesis 47:23.

It is in this environment that later on, in the post-Joseph era, Pharaoh can successfully implement his own policy initiative. In a climate which endorses slavery and has provided him with totalitarian authority, Pharaoh meets no opposition to his plan to enslave the Jewish people. We are arguing that there is a clear link between the Egyptian people's willingness to sell themselves into slavery in Genesis and their acceptance of Pharaoh's plan to enslave Joseph's descendants in Exodus.

Before concluding this section, it is helpful to discuss an argument that can be offered to counter our claim that Joseph's policy initiative was a failure. A simple argument in his favor is that the policy *worked*. As a direct result of Joseph's policy, the people of Egypt and the surrounding areas were saved from what would have been a tragic famine. Joseph, a benevolent leader with no personal ambition, establishes a temporary program to counteract an emergency situation.

That Joseph is a benevolent leader is obvious. However, the policy is not a temporary one, as the text makes plain. In a situation where more and more power is situated at the center, the likelihood is that the power will not be surrendered easily. Joseph's benevolent temporary program, although it was effective, is transformed into the post-Joseph Pharaoh's evil permanent program.

An alternative economic program which publicized the information would have also worked, but at a much-reduced cost. The program might have still incorporated a centralized solution, but also should have recognized the role that the private economy— made up of thousands of individuals competing with one another—can play. By publicizing the information and allowing people to trade in full knowledge of the economic forecast, Pharaoh's power would have been severely limited. An interesting midrashic commentary cited by Rashi claims that, indeed, Joseph did publicize the information. Rashi writes as follows:

> He [Pharaoh] asked them, "Why did you yourselves not lay up corn? Did he [Joseph] not publicly announce that years of famine were coming?" They [the Egyptians] answered him, "We gathered in much, but it has rotted." He said to them, "If this be so, then what he saith to you, do. See, he laid a decree upon the produce and it rotted; what will happen if he lays a decree upon us that we should die!"

Rashi's position, while it resolves the issue of inside information, leaves us with the even more perplexing question of why Joseph "laid a decree upon the produce," a policy that would have an even more pernicious effect than the more passive policy of withholding information.

The policy was effective in another sense as well. How would the conflict between Joseph and his brothers have been resolved had Joseph chosen a different policy? If he had publicized the information, perhaps his brothers would have prepared for the eventual famine and would not have needed to go down to Egypt. Is Joseph playing off the welfare of the Egyptian people (and ultimately the welfare of his own descendants) to resolve the family conflict? While this question, no matter how one resolves it, is beyond the scope of our analysis here, the point that Joseph's plan is bad economics is not at issue.

The road to serfdom is often a direct one. Joseph's policy initiatives, from a purely economic view, are disastrous. There were alternatives, roads not taken. Had Joseph publicized his inside information and chosen either a free-market solution or a mixed-economy solution (a combination solution that incorporated both free-market and collectivist elements), he could have prevented Egypt from becoming the slave state it eventually became.

Joseph and His Brothers

Inside information is a concept that can be applied to a purely economic setting, as in the case above, and to more general settings. Information asymmetries (inside information) can arise in any situation that involves human relationships. Abraham, for example, has inside information vis-à-vis Pharaoh concerning his relationship with his wife/sister Sarah. The example that we will examine here is Joseph's inside information concerning his identity. Joseph knows that he is Joseph, but his brothers do not. The traditional understanding of this narrative is that Joseph uses his informational advantage to offer his brothers a chance for true repentance. The interpretation offered here does not contradict this view but rather deals with the question of when Joseph's inside information becomes public (thereby ceasing to be inside information). According to the *peshat* (literal interpretation), it would appear that the information does not become public until Joseph formally reveals himself. The Torah states: "Then Joseph could not refrain himself before all them that stood by him; and he called, `Let every man go out from me.' And there stood no man with him, while Joseph made himself known unto his brethren" (Genesis 45:1–2). The position taken here is that it is *plausible, and perhaps even likely*, that Judah learns Joseph's identity even before this formal revelation.

What if any textual evidence supports this alternative reading? The first piece of evidence is that Joseph in Genesis 37:6–7, long before these events, told his brothers to be aware that an episode of this kind would occur. How so?

> And he [Joseph] said unto them, "Hear, I pray you, this dream which I have dreamed: For, behold, we were binding sheaves in the midst of the field, and lo, my sheaf arose, and also placed itself upright; and, behold, your sheaves surrounded, and prostrated themselves to my sheaf."

Joseph, at the outset, tells them that one day they will bow down to him. If we assume that the brothers believed the dream, then from the very beginning they were probably on the alert as to how and when it would finally be realized.

It is clear from explicit statements in the Torah that when they first meet Joseph in Egypt, the brothers do not know his identity. For example: "And they [the brothers] knew not that Joseph understood them; for the interpreter was between them. And he turned away from them, and wept" (Genesis 42:23–24). However, almost immediately Joseph begins to signal his identity. Verse 24 continues: "and he returned to them again, and spoke to them, and took from them Simeon, and bound him before their eyes." Rashi explains that it was Simeon who had cast him into the pit many years earlier. Surely the brothers must have wondered why the viceroy chose Simeon, among all the brothers.

Joseph, the story continues, "restores every man's money into his sack" (Genesis 42:25). The brothers, upon discovering the money, react by declaring, "What is this that God has done unto us?" (Genesis 42:28). Aware of the danger of having the money in their possession, the brothers seem to interpret it as a punishment from God, perhaps a punishment for what they did to their brother Joseph many years before.

Even after they are forced to return to Egypt, however, it would appear that they have not made the connection. "And the men [brothers] were afraid, because they were brought into Joseph's house; and they said, `Because of the money that was restored in our bags previously are we brought in'" (Genesis 43:18). The verse explains that they were afraid because of the money, for it appeared as if they had stolen it. By specifying that the reason for their fear was the money, the verse implies that they do not know Joseph's identity. Had they known Joseph was masterminding this entire scheme, their fear would have been directed at him, and not the money.

Joseph immediately drops another hint. He asks the brothers, "Is there peace with your father, the old man of whom you spoke? Is he yet alive?" (Genesis 43:27). Is the viceroy merely engaging in small talk with them? Is that what the brothers assume? Or do they begin to wonder once again?

An even stronger hint follows: "And they sat before him, the firstborn according to his birthright, and the youngest according to his youth: and the men marveled one at another" (Genesis 43:33). Rashi adds that Joseph even calls out their names, one by one. At this point, it is not certain whether the brothers have learned their brother's identity, but it is clear that Joseph is making an attempt to communicate with them.

Does the text itself ever indicate that the brothers do, in fact, catch on? In the middle of chapter 44 we read of Judah's plea on behalf of Benjamin. Joseph's missing silver goblet is found in Benjamin's bag. It appears that the viceroy will take revenge and enslave him. In response, Judah formulates an impassioned prayer. A close reading of these verses implies that at least Judah, of all the brothers, may know Joseph's true identity.

One would expect Judah's plea to include some mention of Benjamin's innocence, yet it does not. He offers only two arguments: (1) "God has found out the iniquity of thy servants" (Genesis 44:16), and (2) "It shall come to pass, when he [Jacob] seeth that the lad is not with us, that he will die: and thy servants shall bring down the gray hairs of thy servant our father with sorrow to the grave" (Genesis 44:31).

Both arguments would be irrelevant to an Egyptian. An Egyptian official would answer the first point by saying, "Who is this god of yours? What do I care about your petty sins and your trivial repentance?" As for the second argument, Judah mentions the word "father" fourteen times during his speech, and it would be hard to understand this repetition unless he knows that his father is also Joseph's father. If Judah is trying to influence an Egyptian viceroy, his speech is too personal and intimate to be effective. Judah's speech is a magnificent and powerful oration precisely because it is directed *at one who is his brother*. The speech, delivered from the heart, is carefully crafted to reach and influence Joseph.

Analyzed from the perspective of inside information, a new understanding emerges. Judah's impassioned speech becomes more humane, given that he has understood Joseph's hints and therefore knows to whom he is talking. Joseph demonstrates through the many signals he sends that he wants to be recognized. Judah picks up on these signals, understands his brother, and sees who he is. He begs Joseph to return Benjamin.

Judah does not know whether Joseph will forgive the family. But at least the two brothers are talking not *at* each other as strangers, but *to* each other as brothers. Judah verbally acknowledges, directly to his brother Joseph, the sin which he and the other brothers committed. Further, he implores him, if he will not forgive the entire family, at least to return Benjamin for the sake of *our* aging father.

In response to this deeply moving scene, Joseph can no longer restrain himself. He is moved finally to end the charade and formally acknowledge his true identity. "And Joseph said unto his brethren, `I am Joseph; doth my father yet live?'" (Genesis 45:3). Joseph, the *zaddik*, accepts Judah's powerful words and embraces his brothers in forgiveness. Joseph hears the strength of Judah's words because Judah himself hears the echo of Joseph's cries.

Conclusion

This chapter has examined two major incidents revolving around Joseph's use of inside information. The first concerns Joseph's public policy prescription. He chooses a policy of centralization in which he does not publicize his inside information. Evaluating it in purely economic terms, the policy is a failure because it leads to the creation of a slave state. A close reading of the biblical verses bears out this interpretation. The second incident relates to Joseph's informational advantage over his brothers. By using the concept of inside information to explore this narrative, an alternative explanation and understanding is uncovered. Judah's speech on behalf of his brothers is offered in full knowledge of his brother's identity.

This chapter differs from the other material included in this book. Most importantly, it demonstrates the importance of attempting to interpret not only legal documents, but also the numerous narrative texts that make up the totality of the received Jewish tradition. In this way, a more complete picture of Jewish business ethics emerges.

8

Jewish Business Ethics in a Pluralistic Society

Jewish business ethics can be viewed in one of two ways. First, it can be treated as a purely theoretical and intellectual exercise. One can study Jewish business ethics to gain a proper understanding of historical Jewish sources related to business and economics. Such an approach is easily justified by the fundamental Jewish obligation to study Torah.

Aaron Levine's *Economic Public Policy and Jewish Law* (1993) best exemplifies this approach. At the outset of the book, Levine carefully notes that his purpose is to articulate an idealistic vision suitable for a purely halakhic state. In his exact words, "This work will focus on economic public policy for a society which is bound by Halakhah (Jewish law). Throughout this work we will refer to this society as the Torah society" (p. 3). A review of his work demonstrates the integrity and worth of such an approach. He paints an inspiring, carefully thought out, well reasoned, and compelling picture, consistent with Jewish legal sources. He explores issues of minimum wage legislation, comparable worth, insider information, and other critical contemporary concerns. Typical of Levine's quest is the following question about comparable worth. Levine wonders, "Does the principle of *darkhei no'am* [lit. ways of peace] . . . require that the legislative body of the Torah society accommodate the demands of this movement as a means of quieting dissension and ill-feeling?" (p. 61). Further along, Levine suggests and demonstrates that "in the Torah society full employment and price stability are mandated goals for the public sector" (p. 201).

Given Levine's stated goal and his final product, one may describe his work as utopian in the best sense of the word. By contrast, Jewish business ethics can be treated as a practical enterprise. From this alternative perspective, the initial question is not a hypothetical one about how business would be conducted in an ideal halakhic world, but rather, how Jewish sources can inform the business ethics debate given the realities of the modern situation, realities which obviously do not conform to Levine's explicit assumption of a Torah society. If this approach is correct, Jewish business ethics is not only an academic exercise, but ideally will provide useful models for business men and women to emulate.

However, if the practical approach, as advocated here, is to make sense, one needs to confront the issue of pluralism head-on. Given the reality that neither the state nor the corporation is a Torah institution, what role is there for religious values to play? The traditional answer has been that religious teachings can guide the individual business man or woman, but have virtually no role to play at the level of the organization or state (at least under current political and social conditions). This final chapter suggests that another, very different answer is possible. Religious sources, and in particular Jewish source, can teach us much about how business enterprises should be organized. Pluralism does not necessarily entail the rejection of traditional sources. Quite the contrary, a return to and an appropriate interpretation of our ethical inheritance are necessary first steps to the continued development of a flourishing pluralistic society.

In chapter 3, it was noted that given the Bible's understanding of the dual nature of man, it is not surprising that its business-related texts embody two sets of norms. The first set of norms were described as legalistic, and the second as models of aspiration. Legalistic norms are unambiguous and specific, and are predominately couched as prohibitions. The motivation for acceptance is the fear of God rather than the love of God. By contrast, models of aspiration are open-ended, more ambiguous, and usually formulated in the positive. The essential characteristic of the models of aspiration is love of our fellow man, even the stranger. The difference between legalistic norms and models of aspiration is most explicit in the writings of Walter Wurzburger. He says (1994, p. 15),

> I deliberately avoid the term *"Halakhic Ethics,"* preferring to speak of "covenant Ethics." In my view, Jewish ethics encompasses not only outright *halakhic* rules governing the area of morality, but also intuitive moral responses arising from the covenantal relationship with God, which provides the matrix for forming ethical ideals not necessarily patterned after legal models.

The main point of this concluding chapter is that it is precisely to these Jewish sources documenting "intuitive moral responses . . . not necessarily patterned after legal models"—models of aspiration—that a practical Jewish business ethicist must, of necessity, turn.

What Is Pluralism?

Most importantly, a pluralistic order is radically different from all traditional conceptions of society, including those conceptions assumed by traditional Jewish sources. A fundamental distinction between a pluralistic society and traditional societies is the formal divorce between moral-cultural institutions (e.g., press, universities, religious institutions) from the apparatus of the state. Further, a pluralistic society separates its economic institutions (at least, to a first approximation) from both the state and the moral-cultural institutions. Michael Novak (1982, p. 56) describes pluralistic societies as follows:

> It is a distinctive invention of democratic capitalism to have conceived a way of differentiating three major spheres of life, and to have assigned to each relatively autonomous networks of institutions. This differentiation of systems sets individuals possessed of the will-to-power on three separate tracks. Political activists may compete for eminence in the political system, economic activists in the economic system, religious activists and intellectuals in various parts of the moral-cultural system. But the powers of each of the three systems over the others, while in each case substantial, are firmly limited.

A great benefit of living in a pluralistic society as described by Novak is the high degree of freedom that characterizes it. Business organizations in pluralistic societies comprise people of all kinds from all parts of the world. Business partners need not worship in the same synagogue or church, or worship at all, for that matter. Customers can focus exclusively on the quality and price of the merchandise purchased rather than concern themselves with the personal values of vendors. Employees need not agree with employers about the true nature of God. In spite of the huge cultural differences between them, countries from everywhere in the world can engage in mutually beneficial trade. One example is sufficient. It comes as no surprise to anyone to read in *Business Week* (Oct. 23, 1995, p. 18) that a Canadian Orthodox Jewish businessman, Paul Reichmann, is now a partner with the Tisch family, fund manger Michael F. Price, banker Edmond Safra, and Saudi Prince Alwaleed bin Talal bin Abdulaziz Alsaud in London's Canary Wharf real estate development project.

The benefits of such freedom in the economic sphere are huge and are often taken for granted (although presumably not by businessmen like Paul Reichmann). Imagine for a moment what life would be like if an employer were to query prospective employees about the details of their religious beliefs and reject job applications on purely religious grounds. An employer might ask, "Do you believe in an afterlife? All of our employees must accept this belief to work here." Obviously, any business or political entity so organized would be consigned to oblivion. On the assumption that such questions have no place in the modern corporation, the freedom inherent in pluralistic societies would seem, then, to be a necessary condition for modern organizations and economies to exist and function.

Whether or not one embraces pluralism as the ideal, if there is to be a relevant religious business ethics it needs to begin by acknowledging the existence and current reality of pluralism. For sure, even without acknowledging pluralism, one could continue to critique business from a religious perspective. But such an approach is necessarily excluded from the business ethics debate, where the ultimate goal is to provide practical advice and useful models for business men and women. Business people, through their decision to enter the world of commerce, have accepted the tenets of pluralism (if only implicitly). Business ethicists, even those working from a religious perspective, if they are to communicate meaningfully with business people, must follow suit.

Pluralistic organizations provide no space (except at the individual level) for legal norms derived from religious texts or authorities. Obviously, within the confines of the board room, it is inappropriate for a business executive to cite a religious law as authoritative. Colleagues, even deeply religious colleagues, would be perplexed, to say the least. The language of religiously based legal norms is properly excluded from pluralistic institutions. Novak, writing from a Catholic perspective similarly states (p. 67), "Those who wish the social order to be based upon commanded `substantive' morality cannot be in favor of pluralism." Simply put, at the institutional level (with the exception of religious institutions), religiously derived legal norms have no status. Some readers may find this diagnosis rather pessimistic.

Therefore, we emphasize what this finding does not suggest. It does not suggest that because some religious language is to be excluded, all religious language is to be excluded.

In chapter 1, we stated that the core problem of business ethics is how best to accommodate the often-conflicting need for individual freedom with the constant demand for responsibility. Here we suggest that one way to resolve this seemingly impossible contradiction is by carefully invoking models of aspiration rather than relying solely on legal models derived from religious teachings. In fact, models of aspiration, grounded in religious sources, are fully consistent with and even promote and support pluralistic institutions.

Models of Aspiration In A Pluralistic World

Models of aspiration, unlike legal norms, are not coercive. One can promote models of aspiration and at the same time fully endorse religious, political, and economic freedom. The appeal, if there is an appeal, is intrinsic to the text or the norm itself. For example, in chapter 2, it was suggested that one of the main reasons we fail at business ethics is an overemphasis on, and inappropriate use of, the rational model of decision making. We argued that most business curriculums teach students to view decisions almost exclusively as opportunities to maximize self-interest. In many cases this strategy is well warranted, but like any ideology, when taken to an extreme, the ideology of rational decision making can lead to perverse and undesirable results.

Important business decisions can also be framed as religious and ethical decisions. Our use of rabbinic material, specifically the midrash related to the idea of *na'aseh v'nishma*, is intended as a powerful illustration of an alternative mode of decision making. The use of the rabbinic material is decidedly not invoked as a specific legal norm. The intention of chapter 2 is not to present a coercive argument, but rather to illustrate and document an alternative way of thinking about decision making. There is an unstated element of religious faith inherent in this approach. Merely presenting and understanding the rabbinic material is sufficient for persuasion. In other words, it is our belief that models of aspiration speak for themselves.

Similarly, in chapter 4, we suggested that the notion of *kofin al midat s'dom* is an appropriate ethical criterion, even in a pluralistic corporation. Recall that in talmudic law, by invoking the *kofin* principle, A can be compelled to surrender a legal right in order to improve B's lot, assuming no cost to A. As in chapter 2, the implicit argument in favor of the contemporary acceptance of the *kofin al midat s'dom* principle is independent of the authoritative nature of the document from which it derives. A religious ethicist may understand his obligation as an interpretation of God's command, but fully recognizes that the acceptance of the principle can be founded on independent grounds. A strong argument in favor of *kofin al midat s'dom* can be established on the basis of utilitarianism, which states that one has an obligation to choose those actions which maximize the welfare of society. Just as utilitarians and Kantians participate in the business ethics debate with no apologies, so too do religious ethicists.

In addition to their noncoercive nature, a second necessary characteristic of models of aspiration is the fact that they are universal in scope. It would be completely inappropriate, for example, to discover suddenly that *kofin al midat s'dom* applies only to selected groups of people, and is not fully general in application. If it were demonstrated that the principle of waiving one's legal rights only applies to fellow Jews, the principle would be of virtually no use in a modern business enterprise, and surely would be of no help to business ethicists. Since the name of the principle invokes the people of Sodom, and therefore carries with it an implicit criticism of their social practices, it is almost impossible to argue that the principle relates only to Jews.

Third, models of aspiration speak directly to current problems. The discussion in chapter 4, for example, invoking both Rabbi Joseph Soloveitchik's concept of *teshuvah* and Michael Walzer's concept of social transformation, relates specifically to the need of modern business ethics to deal with the issues of character development and organizational transformation. Chapter 6 emphasizes one of the most perplexing problems in modern business ethics. The purpose of the chapter is to review the contemporary debate about corporate social responsibility and to suggest a way of moving it beyond the current stalemate. Specifically, we argue that the concept of *lifnim mishurat hadin*, an innovative and ancient Jewish legal doctrine which is usually rendered in English as "beyond the letter of the law," might serve as a model for modern legal and social thought. In chapter 6, we examine talmudic and post-talmudic sources which apply this concept to the area of business ethics, and explore its applicability to the modern situation. Although the business ethics literature rarely refers to talmudic and rabbinic sources, these texts reflect a sophisticated understanding of business practices and ethical problems. The talmudic text cited in the chapter is presented neither as a coercive document nor as a parochial one limited to Jewish interests, but as a nuanced model worthy of contemporary emulation, especially in a pluralistic context. Once again, the belief is that the source speaks for itself. An essential point of the chapter is that the concept of *lifnim mishurat hadin*, or something very much like it, is a necessary principle in a modern economy. Religiously-based sources therefore, far from having no place in the modern corporation, can serve an important function in supporting pluralistic institutions.

If models of aspiration are to speak directly to current problems, the approach must be integrative. One must confront the existing literature "out there" with respect and dignity. Among other things, this necessarily implies that no one religious or philosophical approach has a monopoly on truth. To say, for example, that religious interpretations cannot be influenced by secular approaches is once again tantamount to removing oneself from the business ethics debate. The willingness to openly accept the integrative approach represents another aspect of religious faith. Advocates of the integrative approach certainly can produce no final knock-down proof to show the consistency between religious truths and truths derived on independent grounds. The best one can hope to do is to bring concrete examples which support Norman Lamm's (1990, p. 236) formulation of the *Torah U'Madda* project: "Complementarity offers rousing support to the comprehensiveness of the whole approach. Torah, faith, religious learning on one side, and Madda, science, worldly knowledge on the other, together offer us a more overarching and truer vision than either set alone."

To this point we have suggested that religiously based models of aspiration are noncoercive, universal, and speak directly to current problems. By contrast, legal norms derived from religious teachings are coercive, potentially parochial, and blind to fundamental issue of pluralism. Models of aspiration provide a necessary groundwork for pluralistic organizations. Care should be taken, however, to emphasize that the argument does not imply that legal norms have no role to play whatsoever. First, legal norms, with their precise, uncompromising, and contractual language, provide a moral minimum for the individual. Nothing said to this point should be taken to imply that legal norms should be completely excluded from discussions about business ethics as related to the responsibilities of the individual. The argument thus far suggests that with regard to organizational ethics, legal norms enjoy no special authoritative status. Second, and in spite of the very last point, legal norms can still usefully "inform" the business ethics debate and thus play a crucial role. The same text might be interpreted as simultaneously both legalistic (and thus appropriate at the level of the individual) and aspirational.

Invoking a text in the modern pluralistic corporation or in the public square necessarily implies that we understand and view it, at the moment, as aspirational. A good example of this might be (Deuteronomy 25:13–16). In chapter 3 we suggested that this text, with its precise and unambiguous formulation, provided a good example of a legalistic business-related text.

> Thou shalt not have in thy house diverse measures, a great and a small. A perfect and just weight shalt thou have;

a perfect and just measure shalt thou have; that thy days may be long upon the land which the Lord thy God giveth thee. For all that do such things, even all that do unrighteously, are an abomination unto the Lord thy God.

We now suggest that this same text might also be interpreted as an a model of aspiration, pregnant with meaning relevant for the modern corporation. Consider the following suggestion about how companies should formulate their financial accounting disclosure decisions. Given the reticence of accounting researchers about offering "practical" advice, the discussion of this issue by Baruch Lev (1992) is of great interest. He suggests that the decision to disclose or not to disclose a given piece of information should be made solely in terms of a cost-benefit analysis. His simple rule can be restated as follows: If the benefits (to the organization) from disclosure outweigh the costs (to the organization), disclose; otherwise, don't disclose. He labels his program an "Information Disclosure Strategy." Lev (1992, p. 10) further elaborates:

> Most importantly, disclosure activity does not differ in principle from other corporate activities, such as investment, production, and marketing. Disclosure shares with these activities the fundamental characteristics of providing benefits and incurring costs, and it therefore warrants the careful attention and long-term planning accorded to any major corporate activity. Hence the need for an information disclosure strategy.

He concludes his paper by summarizing (p. 28):

> Information disclosure is not inherently different from other corporate activities such as investment, production, and marketing, and it shares with such activities the fundamental characteristics of promising benefits and incurring costs.

A number of highly controversial implications follow from Lev's assertion that information disclosure "is not inherently different from other corporate activities." For example, he specifically suggests the following "biased" accounting policy (p. 20):

> The financial reports of companies are the prime source of information for those looking for abnormally high profitability, market share gains, and other "suspect" corporate activities. This suggests the advisability of following a well-planned disclosure policy, such as the use of "conservative" (income depressing) accounting techniques. . . . Such an intervention-deterrent disclosure policy is particularly important for companies in politically-sensitive industries such as pharmaceutical, oil and gas, and utilities.

Or, to take a second example, Lev (p. 24) seems to approve of the following observation: "Sometimes, accounting techniques are aimed at portraying a favorable managerial performance intended to affect takeovers or proxy contests." Self-interested managers need to hide their abnormally high profits to avoid unwanted regulation. At other times, they have incentive to portray a "favorable managerial performance" to avoid hostile takeovers. It is not our point to discuss whether these statements are true descriptions of what actually occurs, but rather we question them as normative prescriptions. Are these suggestions consistent with the release of timely, high-quality information? Would an organization that implemented Lev's information-disclosure strategy be satisfying its ethical responsibilities?

Elsewhere it has been suggested that Lev's strategy violates norms of corporate social responsibility (Pava and Krausz 1995). The argument there suggested that managers have a direct responsibility to shareholders to disclose information in an open and neutral way. The withholding of information from shareholders is often tantamount to causing them direct financial harm. Further, there is a high degree of consensus among all stakeholders, but especially among individual shareholders, concerning the importance of neutral financial disclosures (Epstein and Pava 1993).

Strengthening the argument in favor of neutral disclosure by invoking the biblical promise of the existence of a "perfect and just measure" (Leviticus 19:36) does not do violence to the notion of pluralism. To many it adds a dimension of meaning to the discussion. Can Lev's proposal to choose accounting principles that either lower or increase reported net income depending on the perceived political effects be reconciled with the Bible's idea of a "just measure"? If the text is viewed as noncoercive and universal, it can serve an important inspirational function, even if it is also simultaneously interpreted as a "command" at the level of the individual. If nothing else, knowledge and awareness of the biblical material provide evidence that there are other ways to think about how to make decisions, even in business settings. The biblical material reminds us that responsibilities, at least hypothetically, can overwhelm self-interest. Oftentimes it seems that business men and women are simply unaware of any alternatives to the self-interest model. Introducing the biblical material can also serve to underscore the fundamental importance of the issue. In this case, self-consciously and creatively linking the biblical prohibition of diverse measures to the issue of financial disclosure emphasizes its unique and central importance to business ethics.

The integrative approach, which puts models of aspiration at the center, as advocated in this book, can be criticized on the grounds that in the final analysis we cannot conclude with a simple list of "thou shalts" and "thou shalt nots." To many, the final product of a business ethics advertising itself as Jewish must necessarily be a list of legal prescriptions. That is clearly not the intention here. The point of this last chapter is that definitive lists have no place in the modern business context. Jewish business ethics should be thought of as a process of interpretation and not as a final product.

Critics will point out that there is no guarantee that discussing business ethics will lead to an improvement in practice. The approach advocated here, they will say, is too risky. It relies too heavily on the presumed integrity of individual choice. There is no doubt there these critics will be correct. But, given the realities of modern business, what is the alternative to discussion and interpretation? Where are the guarantees? If there is a risk-free approach, an approach that can produce the once-and-for-all definitive business ethics, the onus is on the critics to produce it.

Critics will further suggest that models of aspiration may not speak for themselves, as we "naively" assume. Business ethics must be hard-nosed. We must clearly, unequivocally, and authoritatively articulate the boundaries of acceptable and unacceptable behavior. The only way to affect behavior, according to this view, is to alter the material incentives. If an action is wrong, make the actor pay for it. Inspirational texts will have no impact in the world of business. This criticism is disturbing, especially when it is advanced by religious thinkers. The criticism, in essence, assumes that business men and women are motivated solely by self-interest. Religious thinkers who criticize business ethics as naive reveal a contradictory view of human nature at odds with the majority of their own religious texts. The criticism suggests that human beings are imprisoned by self-interest. The Torah, time and again, suggests otherwise.

Undoubtedly, there are more serious criticisms. Key concepts discussed in this book need more precise definitions. Legal norms, models of aspiration, and the difference between these two categories must be more sharply delineated. As careful as we have tried to be in providing clear examples of each category, the text does not provide precise definitions. Although a healthy ambiguity may at times be useful in stimulating further debate and discussion, more explicit definitions are called for.

The boundaries between the individual and the organization need to be more carefully mapped out, especially given the view here that legal norms are excluded from pluralistic organizations. Certainly huge corporations like IBM, Johnson & Johnson, and General Motors are pluralistic organizations. But what about small privately held corporations and partnerships? Intuitively, our sense is that even the smallest organization—a sole-practitioner medical practice, for example—is still an organization. Nevertheless, a one-size-fits all attitude toward business ethics is problematic. This issue needs further clarification.

Further, and most importantly, the concept of pluralism needs more thorough and systematic exploration. The notion of pluralism and its place within a full-blown Jewish business ethics remains fuzzy. It is not clear whether pluralism is something that religious business ethicists can fully endorse or whether it is a stance adopted to meet the temporary conditions of modern society. The minimalist position thus far put forth holds that it is a reality to be dealt with. Whether one likes it or not, pluralism is a fact on the ground. This view is not fully adequate. Religious thinkers (and business ethicists) who take social issues seriously need to carefully consider how best to justify pluralism. Rather than relying on a minimalist view that simply takes it as a given, religious ethicists must offer innovative interpretations of our traditional teachings in support of pluralism. The maximalist position would provide clear guidance on both why and how we can best promote a pluralism consistent with religious teachings. The task of the hour is to understand how best to accommodate the often-conflicting need for individual freedom with the constant demand for responsibility. Solutions that do not include pluralism are woefully inadequate.

Far from demonstrating that the approach advocated here is not workable, these criticisms provide an agenda for future research. In spite of the fact that clear definitions are difficult to formulate, the notion of models of aspiration, with its deep roots firmly grounded in traditional sources, is clearly recognized as something other than a purely legal approach. Our suggestion that it is now time to harvest its fruits comes with clear and unequivocal suggestions. Similarly, the fact that it is not always easy to distinguish between the individual and the organization does not imply that it is never easy to make the distinction. In fact, in most cases the differences are easily intuited. Even if the notion of pluralism remains hazy, the tangible benefits that pluralistic systems have yielded are crystal-clear.

Conclusion

Diverse voices demand a complete purge of religious language from pluralistic organizations. At one end of the spectrum, there are those who argue that business is a value-free enterprise. As such, religious language, which is decidedly not value-free, can make no positive contribution. This view usually crowns self-interest as the sovereign authority by which to judge business decisions. At the opposite end of the spectrum, there are those who equate religious language with legal norms. They deny the very possibility of models of aspiration. This view can never endorse pluralism. It, therefore, provides little or no practical guidance to business men and women, who by virtue of their decision to enter the world of commerce, necessarily must embrace pluralism. If Judaism only speaks in terms of commandments, there is no entry into the modern business ethics debate.

Regardless of its basis, the suggestion that a religiously grounded business ethics is inappropriate comes at too high a price. It asks us to ignore thousands of years of accumulated wisdom (Berger 1970). It directs us to overlook innumerable practical business examples and solutions. Finally, and most importantly, it charges us to blind ourselves to even the possibility of transcendence.

Abraham Joshua Heschel (1951, p. 3) poetically warns about the limitations inherent in contemporary society's all-embracing focus on material well-being.

> To gain control of the world of space is certainly one of our tasks. The danger begins when in gaining power in the realm of space we forfeit all aspirations in the realm of time. There is a realm of time where the goal is not to have but to be, not to own but to give, not to control but to share, not to subdue but to be in accord. Life goes wrong when the control of space, the acquisition of things of space, becomes our sole concern.

In many modern businesses, life has gone wrong. If we can admit this, perhaps the attempt to integrate traditional religious teachings with the language of business can begin to help set things right.

BIBLIOGRAPHY

Ainslie, George. 1985. "Beyond Microeconomics: Conflict Among Interests in a Multiple Self as a Determinant of Value." In *The Multiple Self*, ed. Jon Elster, pp. 133–175. Cambridge: Cambridge University Press.

Akerlof, George A. 1983. "Loyalty Filters." *American Economic Review* 73, no. 1: 54–63.

————. 1970. "The Market for `Lemons': Quality Uncertainty and the Market Mechanism." *Quarterly Journal of Economics* 84:488–500.

Becker, Gary S. 1976. *The Economic Approach to Human Behavior*. Chicago: University of Chicago Press.

Benston, George J. 1982. "Accounting and Corporate Accountability." *Accounting, Organizations and Society* 7, no. 2: 87–105.

Berger, Peter L. 1970. *A Rumor of Angels: Modern Society and the Rediscovery of the Supernatural*. Garden City, N.Y.: Anchor Books.

Berkovits, Eliezer. 1983. *Not in Heaven: The Nature and Function of Halakha*. New York: Ktav.

Berle, Adolf A. 1954. *The 20th Century Capitalist Revolution*. New York: Harcourt, Brace.

———— and Means, Gardiner C. 1933. *The Modern Corporation and Private Property*. New York: Macmillan.

Birnbaum, Philip. 1951. *High Holiday Prayer Book*. New York: Hebrew Publishing Co.

Bowie, Norman E. 1991. "Challenging the Egoistic Paradigm." *Business Ethics Quarterly* 1:1–21.

Buber, Martin. 1958. *I and Thou*. New York: Macmillan.

Camenisch, Paul F. 1986. "On Monopoly in Business Ethics: Can Philosophy Do It All?" *Journal of Business Ethics* 5:433–443.

Carr, Albert Z. 1980. "Is Business Bluffing Ethical?" *Essentials of Business Ethics*, eds. Peter Madsen and Jay Shafritz. New York: Meridian Press.

Clark, J. Maurice. 1916. "The Changing Basis of Economic Responsibility." *Journal of Political Economy* 24:209–229.

De George, Richard T. 1986. "Theological Ethics and Business Ethics." *Journal of Business Ethics* 5:421–432.

Donaldson, Thomas. 1982. *Corporations and Morality*. Englewood Cliffs, N.J.: Prentice-Hall.

Dworkin, Ronald. 1985. *A Matter of Principle*. Cambridge, Mass.: Harvard University Press.

Elster, Jon. 1985. *The Multiple Self*. Cambridge: Cambridge University Press.

Engel, David L. 1979. "An Approach to Corporate Social Responsibility." *Stanford Law Review* 32:1–98.

Epstein, Marc J., and Pava, Moses L. *The Shareholder's Use of Corporate Annual Reports*. Stamford, CT: JAI Press, 1993.

Etzioni, Amitai. 1988. *The Moral Dimension: Toward a New Economics*.New York: Free Press.

Fackenheim, Emil L. 1973. *Encounters Between Judaism and Modern Philosophy: A Preface to Future Jewish Thought*. New York: Basic Books.

Frank, Robert H. 1988. *Passions Within Reason: The Strategic Role of the Emotions*. New York: Norton.

Freeman, R. Edward. 1994. "The Politics of Stakeholder Theory: Some Future Directions." *Business Ethics Quarterly* 4:409–422.

French, Peter A. 1977. "The Corporation as a Moral Person." Paper presented at the Ethics and Economics Conference, University of Delaware.

Friedman, Heshey H. 1985. "Ethical Behavior in Business: A Hierarchical Approach from the Talmud." *Journal of Business Ethics* 4:117–129.

Friedman, Milton. 1962. *Capitalism and Freedom*. Chicago: University of Chicago Press.

———. 1970. "A Friedman Doctrine—The Social Responsibility of Business Is to Increase Its Profits." *New York Times Magazine,* Sept. 13, pp. 32–33, 123–125.

——— and Friedman, Rose. 1980. *Free to Choose*. New York: Avon Books.

Goodpaster, Kenneth E. 1991. "Ethical Imperatives and Corporate Leadership." In *Business Ethics: The State of the Art,* ed. R. Edward Freeman. New York: Oxford University Press.

——— and Mathews, John B. 1982. "Can a Corporation Have a Conscience?" *Harvard Business Review.* January–February.

Gustafson, James. 1984. *Ethics from a Theocentric Perspective.* Vol.2, *Ethics and Theology.* Chicago: University of Chicago Press.

Guth, Werner; Schmittberger, Rolf; and Schwarze, Bernd. 1982. "An Experimental Analysis of Ultimate Bargaining." *Journal of Economic Behavior and Organization* 3:367–388.

Hartman, David. 1985. *A Living Covenant.* New York: Free Press.

———. 1990. *Conflicting Visions: Spiritual Possibilities of Modern Israel.* New York: Schocken Books.

Hayek, F. A. 1944. *The Road To Serfdom.* Chicago: University of Chicago Press.

Hertz, J. H., ed. 1960. *The Pentateuch and Haftorahs: Hebrew Text, English Translation and Commentary.* 2nd ed. London: Soncino Press.

Heschel, Abraham Joshua. 1951. *The Sabbath: Its Meaning for Modern Man.* New York: Farrar, Straus & Giroux.

———. 1955. *God in Search of Man: A Philosophy of Judaism.* New York: Harper & Row.

———. 1965. *Who Is Man?* Stanford: Stanford University Press.

Hirsch, Fred. 1976. *Social Limits to Growth.* Cambridge, Mass.: Harvard University Press.

Horngren, Charles T., and Foster, George. 1987. *Accounting: A Managerial Emphasis.* 6th ed. Englewood Cliffs, N.J.: Prentice-Hall.

Hornstein, Harvey A.; Fisch, E.; and Holmes, M. 1968. "Influence of a Model's Feelings About His Behavior and His Relevance as a Comparison to Other Observers' Helping Behavior." *Journal of Personal and Social Psychology* 10:222–226.

Jensen, Michael C., and Meckling, William H. 1994. "The Nature of Man." *Journal of Applied Corporate Finance* 7, no. 2:4–19.

Jung, Leo. 1978. "The Ethics of Business." In *Contemporary Jewish Ethics,* ed. Menachem Kellner. New York: Sanhedrin Press.

Kahneman, Daniel; Knetsch, Jack L.; and Thaler, Richard. 1986. "Fairness as a Constraint on Profit Seeking: Entitlements in the Market." *American Economic Review* 76:728–741.

Kant, Immanuel. 1938. *The Fundamental Principles of the Metaphysic of Ethics.* Translated with an introduction by Otto Manthey-Zorn. New York: Appleton-Century Co.

Krueger, David A. 1986. "The Religious Nature of Practical Reason: A Way into the Debate." *Journal of Business Ethics* 5:511–519.

Lamm, Norman. 1990. *Torah Umadda: The Encounter of Religious Learning and Worldly Knowledge in the Jewish Tradition.* Northvale, N.J.: Jason Aronson.

Latane, B., and Darley, J. M. 1970. *The Unresponsive Bystander: Why Doesn't He Help?* New York: Appleton-Century-Crofts.

Lauterbach, Jacob Z., ed. and trans. 1961. *Mekilta de-Rabbi Ishmael.* Philadelphia: Jewish Publication Society.

Leahy, John T. 1986. "Embodied Ethics: Some Common Concerns of Religion and Business." *Journal of Business Ethics* 5:465–472.

Leibowitz, Nehama. 1981. *Studies in Bereshit (Genesis) in the Context of Ancient and Modern Jewish Bible Commentary.* Jerusalem: World Zionist Organization.

Lev, Baruch. 1992. "An Information Disclosure Policy." *California Management Review* 34:9–30.

Levine, Aaron. 1980. *Free Enterprise and Jewish Law: Aspects of Jewish Business Ethics.* New York: Ktav, 1980.

———. 1987. *Economics and Jewish Law: Halakhic Perspectives.* Hoboken, N.J.: Ktav.

———. 1993. *Economic Public Policy and Jewish Law.* Hoboken, N.J.: Ktav, 1993.

———. 1994. "Aspects of the Ideology of Capitalism and Judaism." Paper presented at Orthodox Forum, Yeshiva University.

Lichtenstein, Aharon. 1978. "Does Jewish Tradition Recognize an Ethic Independent of Halakha?" In *Contemporary Jewish Ethics,* ed. Menachem Kellner. New York: Sanhedrin Press.

McCann, Dennis P. 1986. "Umpire and Batsman: Is It Cricket to Be Both?" *Journal of Business Ethics* 5:445–451.

McCoy, Bowen. 1990. "The Parable of the Sadhu." *Harvard Business Review* 61 (September–October 1983). Reprinted in *Essentials of Business Ethics,* ed. Peter Madsen and Jay M. Shafritz. New York: Penguin Books.

March, James. 1978. "Bounded Rationality, Ambiguity, and the Engineering Choice." *Bell Journal of Economics* Vol. 9 3:587-608.

———. 1994. With the assistance of Chip Heath. *A Primer on Decision Making: How Decisions Happen.* New York: Free Press.

Marwell, Gerald, and Ames, Ruth E. 1981. "Economists Free Ride, Does Anyone Else?" *Journal of Public Economists* 15:295–310.

Nagel, Thomas. 1986. *The View from Nowhere.* Oxford: Oxford University Press.

Novak, Michael. 1982. *The Spirit of Democratic Capitalism.* New York: Simon & Schuster.

———. 1993. "The Creative Person." *Journal of Business Ethics* 12:975–979.

Nozick, Robert. 1993. *The Nature of Rationality.* Princeton, N.J.: Princeton University Press.

Okun, Arthur M. 1975. *Equality and Efficiency: The Big Tradeoff.* Washington, D.C.: Brookings Institution.

Pava, Moses L., and Krausz, Joshua. 1995. *Social Responsibility and Financial Performance: The Paradox of Social Cost.* Westport, Conn.: Quorom Press.

Peli, Pinchus. 1980. *On Repentance: In the Thought and Oral Discourses of Rabbi Joseph B. Soloveitchik.* Jerusalem: Oroth.

Rodewald, Richard A. 1987. "The Corporate Social Responsibility Debate: Unanswered Questions About the Consequences of Moral Reform." *American Business Law Journal* 25:443–466.

Sacks, Jonathan . 1992. "Creativity and Innovation in Halakah." *Rabbinic Authority and Personal Autonomy,* ed. Moshe Z. Sokol. Northvale NJ: Jason Aronson Inc.

Sears, David O.; Lau, Richard R.; Tyler, Tom R.; and Allen, Harris M., Jr. 1980. "Self-Interest vs. Symbolic Politics in Policy Attitudes and Presidential Voting." *American Political Science Review* 74:670–784.

Shilo, Shmuel. 1980. "*Kofin al Midat S'dom:* Jewish Law's Concept of Abuse of Rights." *Israel Law Review* 15:49–78.

Soloveitchik, Joseph B. 1965. *The Lonely Man of Faith.* New York: Doubleday.

———. 1967. "Confrontation." In *A Treasury of "Tradition",* ed. Norman Lamm and Walter S. Wurzburger, pp. 55–80. New York: Hebrew Publishing Co., 1967.

———. 1983. *Halakhic Man.* Philadelphia: Jewish Publication Society.

Stark, Andrew. 1993. "What's the Matter with Business Ethics?" *Harvard Business Review* Vol. 71, 3:38-48.

Steinsaltz, Adin. 1990. *The Talmud: The Steinsaltz Edition.* New York: Random House.

Stevens, Betsy. 1994. "An Analysis of Corporate Ethical Code Studies: 'Where Do We Go From Here?'" *Journal of Business Ethics* 13:63–69.

Stigler, George J., and Becker, Gary S. 1977. "De Gustibus Non Est Disputandum." *American Economic Review* 67:76–90.

Stone, Christopher D. 1975. *Where the Law Ends: The Social Control of Corporate Behavior.* New York: Harper & Row.

Tamari, Meir. 1987. *With All Your Possessions: Jewish Ethics and Economic Life.* New York: Free Press.

Tversky, Amos, and Kahneman, Daniel. 1981. "The Framing of Decisions and the Psychology of Choice." *Science* 211:453–458.

Walton, Clarence C. 1988. *The Moral Manager.* New York: Harper & Row.

Walzer, Michael. 1983. *Spheres of Justice,* New York: Basic Books.

———. 1985. *Exodus and Revolution.* New York: Basic Books.

———. 1987. *Interpretation and Social Criticism.* Cambridge, Mass.: Harvard University Press.

Watts, Ross, and Zimmerman, Jerold. 1986. *Positive Accounting Theory* Englewood Cliffs N.J.: Prentice-Hall.

Wiesel, Elie. 1976. *Messengers of God: Biblical Portraits and Legends.* New York: Random House.

Wood, Donna J. 1994. *Business and Society,* New York: Harper Collins College Publishers.

Wurzburger, Walter. 1994. *Ethics of Responsibility: Pluralistic Approaches to Covenantal Ethics.* Philadelphia: Jewish Publication Society.

GLOSSARY OF RABBINIC TERMS

Akedah. Binding of Isaac.

Alef, beth, gimmel, dalet. The first four letters of the Hebrew alphabet.

Alenu. Literally, "it is upon us". A prayer recited three times daily by traditional Jews.

Beth Hamidrash. The traditional study house.

Darkhei no'am. Literally, "ways of pleasantness." The goal of achieving harmonious interpersonal relations.

Din. The strict letter of the law, specific legal rulings.

Dinar. A gold or silver coin in the talmudic period.

Eretz Yisrael. The land of Israel.

Gezel. Robbery.

Halakhah. Jewish law.

Hiddush. A creative interpretation of Jewish law.

Kofin Al Midat S'dom. Legal and ethical term literally translated as "one is compelled not to act in the manner of Sodom." The rule overrides one's legal rights where insisting on exercising them brings no benefit and waiving them in a specific situation would be beneficial to another.

Lifnim Mishurat Hadin. Legal and ethical term literally translated as "beyond the letter of the law."

Masorah. Process of transmission or the chain of Jewish tradition.

Midrash. Rabbinic embellishment on a biblical text.

Mitzvah (plural Mitzvot). God's commandment.

Musaf Service. The additional prayer service recited by traditional Jews on Sabbath and Holidays.

Na'aseh v'nishma. Literally, "we will do and we will hear."

Oral Torah. Authoritative interpretation of the written law which was regarded as given to Moses on Sinai and therefore coexistent with the Written Law.

Or-ha-Hayyim. Commentary on the Pentateuch, written by Hayyim ben Moses Attar, rabbi and kabbalist (1693-1743, Morocco).

Peshat. The literal or simple interpretation of a biblical text.

Prosbol. A legal document which allows the lender and borrower to circumvent the cancellation of the debt in the sabbatical year. According to the Talmud the text of the prusbol reads as follows: "I hand over to you, So-and-so, the judges in such-and-such a place, [my bond], so that I may be able to recover any money owing to me from So-and-so at any time I shall desire."

Ramban. Acronym for Nahmanides, Moses b. Nahman, one of the leading authorities of talmudic literature in the middle ages (1194-1270, Spain).

Rashi. Acronym for Solomon b. Isaac, one of the greatest Jewish biblical and talmudic scholars of all time (1040-1105, France).

Rosh. Acronym for the talmudic scholar Rabbi Asher b. Yehiel (1250-1327, Germany, Spain).

Rosh Hashanah. The Jewish New Year.

Sanhedrin. The Jewish high court.

Sh'ma. Literally, hear. Refers to the prayer affirming God's Kingship of the universe.

Sh'mittah. The sabbatical year.

Teshuva. Repentance.

Toroth. Plural for Torah. Refers to the written and oral Torahs.

Tosafists. A school a talmudic commentators following Rashi.

Written Torah. The Jewish bible.

Yishuv Ha'olam. The settlement of the world.

Yom Kippur. The day of Atonement. The holiest day in the Jewish calendar.

Zaddik. A righteous person.

Zuz. A silver coin in the talmudic period, one fourth of a shekel.

INDEX

203